Adam Egger, Peter Dern

101 Remote Collaboration Hacks

Fun, Energy, Trust - How to Connect People in the Virtual World

Contents

Small Hacks, Big Impact

Are you tired of endless and unproductive virtual meetings? Do you struggle to keep yourself and others engaged during remote sessions, and leave feeling frustrated and drained? It doesn't have to be that way.

You can transform your virtual meetings into a fun, energizing, and productive experiences with even just a few of the 101 practical and effective hacks we share. Whether you're a team leader, facilitator, trainer, or simply a participant seeking to improve team spirit, this book is for you.

We believe that good remote collaboration is not just about tools but about effective practices that help build and nurture human connections. As you explore our 101 hacks, you'll learn how to build trust, fun, and energy within your remote team and create a more positive and engaging virtual meeting experience.

Our hacks can be applied to any kind of remote meeting, workshop, training, or conference. And they work no matter the topic - from brainstorming to culture to productivity. We provide real-life examples, expert insights, and actionable tips.

Imagine leaving a remote planning meeting with an actual plan, feeling energized and motivated to put it into action. Imagine you and your team looking forward to your virtual meetings and leaving with a sense of accomplishment. With the help of our book, you can make it happen.

Don't waste any more time on unproductive virtual meetings. Take the first step towards becoming a remote collaboration expert and transform your virtual sessions into a valuable and productive use of everyone's time.

Here's What You Will Learn

This book is designed to be a practical guide that you can use to improve your skills as a facilitator, trainer, coach, or team leader. Our 101 hacks and the bonus material with our favorite remote icebreakers and methods at the end will give you the tips and techniques you need to run more effective meetings and workshops.

Here is what you will learn:

- How to create a safe and inclusive environment in the virtual world where people feel comfortable sharing their thoughts and ideas.

- How to use different remote techniques for different goals, such as brainstorming, decision-making, or problem-solving.

- How to ask the right questions that trigger thought and encourage constructive discussion.

- How to keep the discussion positive while still being realistic and addressing any issues that arise

- Strategies for managing remote group discussion when many people have different opinions or are talking at the same time.

- How to overcome your fear of facilitating, even if you are naturally shy or struggle with positioning yourself as a facilitator.

- Strategies for adapting your existing in-person facilitation skills to remote or virtual meetings, including using technology effectively and managing the unique challenges of online meetings.

- Ways to respond when people are not prepared, including how to adjust your agenda and manage expectations to still achieve your desired outcomes.

- How to structure remote workshop effectively.

- Tips for using checklists to ensure that you do not miss any important steps when facilitating a remote meeting or workshop.

You can read this book cover to cover or jump straight to the hacks that interest you the most. We recommend bookmarking the hacks that are most relevant to your current needs, so you can refer to them when you need a quick refresher.

101 Most Powerful Remote Hacks

From your own experience, you know that remote facilitation comes with its own unique set of challenges. Keeping participants engaged, managing technology, and delivering a high-quality session can be difficult when you are not in the same physical space as your audience.

The benefits of reading this book are numerous. First, you will be able to enhance your moderation and facilitation skills and increase your confidence as a remote facilitator. Each hack is designed to help you overcome a specific challenge or problem that commonly arises in remote workshops. By implementing these hacks, you will be able to deliver workshops that are engaging, interactive, and effective.

Second, you will be able to save time and increase your productivity. Rather than spending hours researching best practices for remote facilitation, you can use this book as a one-stop-shop for all your facilitation needs.

Finally, you will be able to enhance the experience of your participants. By using these facilitation hacks, you will be able to create a workshop that's memorable and the results of which are sustainable and impactful. Participants will leave feeling satisfied and motivated, knowing exactly what to do next. And they will be more likely to recommend your workshop to others.

We discussed at length what the appropriate order should be for the hacks. Chronological order, with respect to when they best apply (i.e., before the workshop, at the beginning, in the middle, or at the end), did not make much sense, as many of the hacks can and should be applied at various stages. Some are also more general in nature and do not fit into a specific flow. Additionally, alphabetical order would be rather arbitrary as well.

As a result, we decided to present the hacks in a random list - which makes reading more enjoyable and surprising. The order has no particular significance, such as the first being the most important. Well, maybe that is not 100% true: our Hack #1, which is about idea generation, is for sure one of the most important ones.

Enjoy reading!

#1 - No Brainstorming, Please

Silence before the Storm: Maximize Workshop Brainpower with this Note-Taking Hack.

Let us face it: brainstorming sucks. Everyone shouting out ideas all at once? More like a chaotic mess than a productive method. If you want to truly maximize the potential input of your workshop attendees, try this simple hack: ask them to take notes in silence first.

By giving participants time to individually gather their thoughts, you will be tapping into the power of introverts and allowing everyone to generate ideas without feeling the pressure of the group. Plus, it helps to eliminate groupthink and biases that can sometimes stifle creativity in a brainstorming session. Once everyone has had a chance to jot down their ideas, you can move on to the group discussion and collaboration phase with a fresh batch of diverse ideas to work with.

For example, if you are leading a workshop on product development, ask everyone to take five minutes to write down all the features they would want in the perfect product on a piece of paper. Then, once everyone has completed their notes, you can begin a discussion on which features are most important and why (e.g., by asking everyone to just present their top 1, most important idea).

So, before you jump right into the brainstorming session, remember the power of silence. Give everyone a chance to gather their thoughts first, and you might just be surprised at the level of creativity that emerges.

Hack #1: Have people note their ideas before collecting and processing them.

#2 - Your Role: Not The Hero

Check Your Ego: Why Being a Hero Won't Make You a Star.

As a facilitator, it is easy to fall into the trap of trying to be the hero of the workshop. You want to be the one who comes up with all the ideas, leads all the discussions, and impresses the participants with your knowledge and expertise. But the truth is, trying to shine like a star can dim the light of your workshop.

This has a huge benefit: By letting go of the need to be the hero, you create a more inclusive and collaborative environment that allows the participants to shine. This approach not only fosters a sense of ownership and engagement among the participants but also leads to better ideas and outcomes.

Instead of dominating the conversation, encourage participants to share their experiences and insights. Use active listening skills to ensure that everyone's ideas are heard and valued. Design activities that allow participants to work together in small groups, so everyone has a chance to contribute. In this way, you will create a safe space for participants to share their views and engage in meaningful discussions that lead to better outcomes.

Hack #2: Do not be the hero.

#3 - Connecting People

Connection Before Content.

Forget about diving into your content straight away. Instead, take the time to build a genuine human connection with your audience before even touching your slides. By creating a welcoming and friendly atmosphere, you'll open up a space of trust and respect that will allow your participants to be more receptive and engaged during the rest of the session.

By prioritizing human connection over content, you'll be able to create a more comfortable and authentic environment that will encourage participation, build rapport, and foster trust among your participants. By doing this, you can set the stage for a more effective and impactful workshop or training session, where participants feel heard, valued, and respected.

Reserve enough time for the connection part. Use some of the icebreakers described at the end of this book. Start off by asking open-ended questions that allow participants to share a little bit about themselves, their backgrounds, and their goals for the session. Encourage group activities that require participants to collaborate and interact with one another, such as icebreakers, team-building exercises, and role-playing scenarios.

By incorporating these elements of connection into your facilitation, you will be able to create a more inclusive and supportive environment that sets the tone for a successful workshop or training session.

Hack #3: Build connections before getting into content.

#4 - Tools And Methods: Less Is More

The Facilitation Swiss Army Knife: Mastering Your Toolkit for Remote Success.

Just like a Swiss Army Knife, a facilitator needs a trusty toolkit of tools and methods that can handle any job in a remote workshop. However, having a million tools will not do much good if you don't know how to use them effectively. That is why it is important to curate your toolkit and focus on the tools that work best for your style and the situation at hand.

By building a robust toolkit of decision-making techniques, problem-solving exercises, ideation methods, and more, you will be prepared to handle any challenge that comes your way in a remote setting. The right tools can help participants collaborate, brainstorm, and generate innovative ideas, all while keeping them engaged and focused.

For example, if you are facilitating a remote brainstorming session with a team of highly visual designers, you might reach for your trusty "Mind Mapping" tool. With this technique, you can guide participants through a visual exploration of ideas and help them organize their thoughts in a structured way. By using a tool that you are familiar with and confident in, you can focus on facilitating the conversation and helping the team achieve their goals.

So, just like a Swiss Army Knife, build a toolkit of versatile tools and methods that can handle any job in a remote workshop. Curate your collection to focus on the tools that work best for you and master them to become a true pro at facilitating remote sessions! Remember, it is not about the quantity of tools in your toolkit, it is about the quality and how effectively you can use them. Doing less better - that is the trick!

Hack #4: Have a small but robust toolkit of exercises and techniques.

#5 - Housekeeping Rules

Buckle Up: Set the Tone for a Great Remote Workshop with a Fun and Casual Housekeeping Routine.

Before launching your remote workshop, it is important to set the tone and establish some ground rules. However, nobody likes to sit through a dry slide with 10 points of dos and don'ts. Not only does this kill every energy, it also can come across stiff and firm. So why not spice things up and add some fun to your housekeeping routine?

Instead of going through a boring list of rules, you can make the housekeeping rules more casual and amusing by using phrases such as "fasten your seatbelts," "switch your mobile devices to flight mode," "put your desk in an upright position," and "get ready for takeoff."

By injecting some humor and personality into your welcome routine, you will not only set a positive tone for the workshop, but you will also create a more relaxed and engaging atmosphere. Your participants will feel more comfortable asking questions and sharing their thoughts, leading to a more productive and enjoyable learning experience.

There are quite a few moderators and facilitators who completely avoid showing or defining housekeeping rules at the beginning because presenting a set of rules to the participants right at the start shifts the mood of a workshop in a more formal direction.

Hack #5: No boring housekeeping rules at the beginning.

#6 - Breakouts Secret 1: Camera-On Effect

Breakout Sessions are Your Secret Weapon to Boosting Camera-on Culture.

Are you tired of talking to a sea of black screens during your virtual meetings and workshops? It is time to ditch the passive audience and activate your participants with a camera-on culture. And the secret to doing so lies in leveraging breakout sessions.

Here is how it works: Instead of asking everyone to keep their cameras on throughout the entire session, use breakouts to create a more intimate setting where participants can connect with each other. When people are given the opportunity to see and interact with their peers in smaller groups, they are more likely to turn on their cameras and engage fully in the activity. And when they return to the main room, the camera-on momentum is likely to continue, resulting in a more energetic and productive group dynamic.

The benefits of this hack are two-fold. Not only does it create a more engaging and interactive virtual environment, but it also fosters a sense of community among participants. By seeing and interacting with each other, people are more likely to feel connected and invested in the outcome of the session.

Try it and see the difference it makes in your virtual meetings and workshops!

Hack #6: Use breakout sessions in virtual workshops to increase the camera-on rate.

#7 - Workshop Invitation

First Impressions Matter: Check Your Invitation to Set the Stage for an Engaging Remote Workshop.

It is easy to overlook the importance of a meeting or workshop invitation, but it can make all the difference in creating a successful event. The title and agenda of your session can set the tone and expectations for your participants.

If your participants do not expect much, and if they know that there is no need for them to contribute, they come with the mindset "ok, let's do some email in parallel". To be honest, not every meeting can be the highlight of the week – there are those status update meetings where everyone is only sitting and listening.

A dull or vague title can leave your attendees disinterested, unengaged, and unmotivated to participate. On the other hand, a catchy and intriguing title can spark curiosity and encourage attendees to show up prepared and excited to engage in the meeting.

The benefit of this hack is that it creates a positive first impression and sets the tone for a successful remote workshop. By using a compelling title and agenda, you can create excitement, set clear expectations, and communicate the value of the meeting to your participants.

This even works for meetings and regular updates. For example, instead of "Team Meeting", try "Brainstorming Bonanza: How to Take Our Team to the Next Level." Or instead of "Project Status Update," try "Showcasing Our Progress: A Visual Tour of Our Project."

In short, by taking the time to craft a thoughtful and engaging invitation, you can set the stage for a productive and engaging remote workshop.

Hack #7: Craft a compelling invitation.

#8 - The First Minutes

Speak up or Shut up: Why the First Minutes of Your Workshop are Crucial.

Have you ever had a workshop where no one seems to want to speak up? It can be frustrating for both the facilitator and the participants. But did you know that the first few minutes of your workshop can make or break the level of engagement for the rest of the session?

Here is a hack to ensure everyone feels heard: start the workshop off with a round of introductions and ask each person "What could you talk about for hours?" Suddenly everyone is eager to share. One person talks about their love of hiking, and someone else chimes in about their favorite camping spots. Another person shares their passion for cooking, and soon everyone is swapping recipes and tips. By the time you move on to the workshop topic, everyone is relaxed, engaged, and ready to participate.

Not only does this hack encourage participation from the get-go, but it also helps to establish a sense of connection among the group. When people feel heard and valued, they are more likely to engage and contribute throughout the rest of the workshop.

Another nice icebreaker that works well if you are leading a team-building workshop, where people already know each other goes like this: ask each participant to share one thing they appreciate about their colleagues. This not only fosters a positive environment but also helps to build trust and rapport among team members.

Remember, if you do not get people speaking up in the first few minutes, they may remain silent for the entire workshop. So, give everyone a chance to speak their mind early on and watch the level of engagement soar.

Hack #8: Let everyone speak in the first minutes.

#9 - Background Used Cleverly

Backdrop beats Boring Slides.

PowerPoint is boring. We all know that. So why not ditch it and make your virtual workshops pop with a simple backdrop hack? Instead of sharing your screen to show slides, use your webcam to project a creative virtual backdrop with relevant content that pops up behind you.

This not only adds visual interest to your presentation, but also keeps your audience focused on you, the facilitator, rather than staring at a screen full of bullet points. Plus, it is a fantastic way to inject some personality and branding into your remote workshops.

For example, if you are running a session on marketing strategies, you could create a custom background image featuring a collage of ads or marketing materials relevant to your audience. Or, if you are hosting a team-building workshop, you could create a backdrop with fun team photos or memes to keep things light and engaging.

By using a customized backdrop as your "slides", you are showing your audience that you are creative, innovative, and willing to think outside the box to keep things interesting. So go ahead, give your boring old PowerPoint the boot, and create a backdrop that truly wows your virtual attendees!

Hack #9: Use your virtual background for content, not only for ambience.

#10 - Play Music

Pump up the volume - Play Music

Playing music is the ultimate facilitation hack that can take your workshops from dull and uninspiring to engaging and energizing in seconds. Not only can it set the tone and create a positive atmosphere, but it can also help to stimulate creativity, increase focus, and reduce stress and anxiety.

At the beginning of a workshop, you can use upbeat and motivational songs to set the tone for the day ahead and energize your participants. During breaks, you can play more relaxing or meditative music to help your participants recharge and refocus. During silent work or breakout sessions, you can use instrumental music to enhance concentration and productivity.

The benefits of playing music are endless. It can help to break the ice and encourage participants to connect with each other, enhance the learning experience, and leave an impression on your participants. Plus, who does not love a good dance break?

For example, if you are running a team-building workshop, you could play "Happy" by Pharrell Williams at the beginning of the day to get everyone in a positive mindset. During a brainstorming session, you could play instrumental music to stimulate creativity and inspire new ideas. And during a reflective exercise, you could play a calming song like "Weightless" by Marconi Union to help your participants relax and reflect.

Incorporating music into your workshops is a simple and effective way to create a dynamic and engaging environment. So, turn up the volume and see the difference it can make!

Hack #10: Play music.

#11 - Timing And Agenda

Ditch the Clock: Why Keeping Your Participants in the Dark About Time is a Game-Changer

Are you tired of leading workshops that feel like a snooze-fest? It is time to switch things up and keep your participants on their toes. Here is a little secret - do not share the agenda with the time allotted for each section or part with the participants. Instead, give them only a high-level outline of the workshop and let the rest unfold organically.

By keeping the participants in the dark about the time allotted for each section or part, you free yourself from being a slave to the clock. This means you can be more flexible and adapt to the needs and interests of your participants. Surprise them with unexpected activities or discussions that you might have had to cut if you were following a strict timeline.

Not revealing the exact time also means that if you have to skip certain elements, participants will not feel like they've been cheated out of what they were promised. They will not be anxiously waiting for the clock to hit a certain time, rather they'll be fully engaged in the present moment.

For example, if you are leading a brainstorming session, provide the group with a high-level outline of the topics you'll be discussing and the overall goal of the session. Then, allow the conversation to flow naturally, without worrying about how much time each topic is taking.

Remember, time is a construct - do not let it control your workshop. Try out this hack and watch as your participants become fully engaged in the present moment.

Hack #11: Do not share the agenda with the time allotted for each section or part with the participants.

#12 - Plan And Reality

The Art of Agile Facilitation: Forget the Plan and Embrace the Flow.

Sure, you may have spent hours crafting the perfect plan for your workshop, but here is a little secret: sometimes, the best thing you can do is throw it out the window. The truth is, no matter how much you prepare, things do not always go according to plan. And that is okay!

The benefit of this hack is that it encourages you to be flexible and adapt to unexpected changes that may arise during your session. By being open to improvisation, you create a more dynamic and engaging environment that can lead to more creative and collaborative results.

For example, imagine you are leading a team-building workshop and your plan is to start with an icebreaker activity to get everyone comfortable. But as soon as you walk into the room, you sense that the energy is off, and people seem tense. Instead of pushing forward with your planned activity, you may want to pivot and start with a check-in question to help address the group's unease.

Remember, being prepared is important, but being able to adapt and respond to the moment is what sets great facilitators apart. So go ahead, toss that plan out the window and see where the journey takes you!

Hack #12: Have a plan. But stay flexible.

#13 - Good Things First

Flip the Script and Start with the Good Stuff.

Forget the typical approach of diving right into the problem-solving mode. Instead, flip the script and start with a positive spin. Begin the session by asking participants what is working, what's already good, or what successes they have had. This approach sets a positive tone, puts everyone at ease, and primes the group to be more open-minded and solution oriented.

By acknowledging and highlighting what's good, participants are more likely to feel appreciated and valued, which builds trust and rapport. This approach also helps shift focus away from problems and towards solutions. Plus, it is an excellent way to get people talking and engaged, and it creates a more inclusive and collaborative environment.

For example, if you are leading a team meeting to discuss a project's issues, start by asking everyone to share their accomplishments or milestones from the past week. You will be surprised how much positivity can come from this simple question. It also gives a chance for people to share their work that might have gone unnoticed in the usual problem-focused discussions.

So, do not be afraid to flip the script and start with the good stuff. Your participants will thank you, and you will be amazed at the results.

Hack #13: If you run a session to solve problems, always start with "what's good", before you enter the problem space.

#14 - Breakouts Secret 2: Raising The Energy

Revive Your Workshop with This Simple Hack: Breakout to Raise the Energy!

Are you tired of running virtual workshops that feel like endless Zoom meetings? Do you struggle to keep your audience engaged and energized? If so, it is time to try this simple but effective hack: use breakouts to raise energy!

Even if your content is compelling, sitting and listening to the same voices for hours on end can be draining. Breakouts give your audience a chance to stretch their legs, connect with peers, and get their blood flowing. Plus, they allow for more diverse perspectives and active participation.

For example, if you are running a training course on effective communication, you might break participants into smaller groups to practice active listening and feedback. Or, if you are facilitating a brainstorming session, you could use breakouts to encourage teams to generate and share new ideas.

The benefits of using breakouts are clear: higher energy, more engagement, and better retention of information. So next time you are planning a virtual workshop, do not underestimate the power of this simple hack. Break out of the traditional format and watch your audience come alive!

Hack #14: Use breakout sessions in virtual workshops to raise the energy level.

#15 - Videos in Breaks

The Power of YouTube: Using Videos to Spice Up Your Workshop Breaks.

Are you tired of seeing your workshop participants scrolling on their phones during breaks? Want to engage them in a fun and interesting way? Look no further than YouTube!

This hack is all about incorporating YouTube videos into your workshop breaks. By playing interesting songs or funny videos, you can help your participants relax, recharge, and refocus for the next session. Not only does this hack help break up the monotony of the workshop, but it also helps build a sense of community and shared experience among your participants.

For example, if you are running a team-building workshop, you could play a hilarious video that highlights the importance of teamwork. Or if you are running a sales training workshop, you could play a motivational song that pumps up your participants and gets them ready to tackle their next sales pitch.

So, what are you waiting for? Start curating your YouTube playlist today and take your workshop breaks to the next level!

Hack #15: Play YouTube videos during breaks.

#16 - Separate Problems From Solutions

Maximize Your Workshop Impact: Separate Problem-Solving and Solution-Finding.

As a facilitator in a virtual environment, it is more important than ever to make sure your workshops are as impactful as possible. One powerful way to achieve this is by separating problem-solving from solution-finding. By doing so, you can ensure that your workshops are efficient, focused, and produce effective solutions that address the root cause of the problem.

In virtual workshops, participants can easily become distracted or disengaged, which can hinder the problem-solving process. By separating the two stages, you can maintain focus and engagement throughout the workshop. This will help you avoid getting bogged down by irrelevant issues and ensure that you produce solutions that are practical and effective.

For example, if you are running a virtual workshop on process improvement, your first step (after a warm-up) would be identifying the specific process-related issues that are causing problems. Once you have fully understood and prioritized these issues, you can then collaborate with your participants to generate potential solutions that address them. By doing this, you can help your participants feel a sense of progress and accomplishment as they move through the workshop.

Remember, the key to effective problem-solving is a thorough understanding of the problem itself. By separating problem-solving from solution-finding, you can maximize the impact of your virtual workshops and help your participants achieve their goals in a dynamic and engaging way!

Hack #16: Separate between problem definition and solution finding. Problems first, solutions second.

#17 - Breakouts Secret 3: Team Size

The Perfect Size for Breakout Rooms: The Goldilocks Principle.

You might think that the size of a breakout room does not matter but let me tell you - it is crucial. In the virtual world, you do not have the luxury of reading body language or using other nonverbal cues to gauge engagement. That is why the perfect size for a breakout session is five participants (or rather 4-6).

Why? Well, too many people and some will get lost in the shuffle, feeling like they cannot contribute or be heard. Too few, and there is a risk of people being left alone if someone has to leave early or encounters technical difficulties. But with 4-6 people, everyone has a chance to share their ideas, listen to others, and build meaningful connections.

So, if you want to ensure that your breakout sessions are engaging and productive, remember the Goldilocks principle - not too big, not too small, but exactly right.

Example: Imagine you are facilitating a virtual brainstorming session for a team of twenty people. Instead of one giant breakout room, you split them into smaller groups of 4-6 participants. Each group is given a clear prompt and a designated breakout room facilitator or moderator to ensure everyone has a chance to share their ideas. As a result, each person can contribute, and the entire team is able to generate a wide range of creative ideas.

Hack #17: Five is the magic number for your virtual breakout sessions.

#18 - Introduction Round

The Power of Choice: Let Your Participants Take the Lead in Introduction Rounds.

Instead of the usual clockwise or random order, let the person speaking choose who goes next. This simple technique gives the power of choice to your participants, making them more invested in the conversation and attentive to what others are saying. Plus, it adds an element of surprise and excitement to the usual routine.

For example, imagine you are facilitating a team-building workshop. You start with an introduction round and ask everyone to share their name, role, and a fun fact. Instead of going in order, you let the first person choose who goes next. Maybe they choose the quiet team member who has not spoken up yet. Or perhaps they pick the team leader to set the tone. Either way, the power of choice creates a more dynamic and engaging experience for everyone.

This technique can be applied to any situation where one person at a time takes their turn. To make sure that no one gets forgotten, write their names on a piece of paper and tick them off after their turn.

So, next time you are leading a workshop, try giving the power of choice to your participants in the introduction rounds. You will be amazed at the difference it can make!

Hack #18: Have the participants define who goes next in round robins like introductions.

#19 - Safe Space

What happens in Vegas, stays in Vegas: Set the Tone for Openness and Vulnerability from the Start.

Creating a safe space for participants is essential for facilitating meaningful and productive workshops. But how can you ensure that everyone feels comfortable enough to share their thoughts and feedback openly, especially in a group of strangers? The answer lies in the warmup phase, which sets the tone for the entire workshop.

The key is to establish a comfort zone from the start. Begin with a quick icebreaker that encourages participants to share something personal or fun about themselves. This not only helps everyone to get to know each other better, but it also creates a sense of connection and trust among the group.

Another effective way to create a safe environment is by setting clear expectations for the workshop. Let everyone know that their thoughts and opinions are valued, and that any feedback given will be received with an open mind. Encourage participants to share their own goals and expectations for the workshop, and to voice any concerns they may have. We often use the slogan that this workshop is like Vegas: "What happens in Vegas, stays in Vegas." People can fool around, experience things without embarrassment, fear, or negative judgment by others.

Finally, be mindful of your own language and behavior as the facilitator. Lead by example and demonstrate openness and vulnerability yourself. Show that it is okay to make mistakes, ask questions, and share your own experiences. This will encourage others to do the same.

Hack #19: Create a safe space right from the start that everyone feels comfortable with.

#20 - Spend More Time On Problems

Flip the Focus: Why Talking More About Problems is the Solution.

In the world of virtual workshops, it is easy to get caught up in finding quick solutions to problems. Virtual workshops are usually shorter than onsite events which tempts us to jump quicker to solutions. But here is the thing: the more time you spend discussing the problem, the better your solution will be.

The reason this approach is effective is because when you spend more time talking about the problem, you're able to fully understand the nuances and complexities of the issue at hand. And in virtual settings where non-verbal cues may be missed or muted, it is important to take extra time to ensure everyone is on the same page before moving on to finding a solution.

So, next time you are facilitating a virtual problem-solving workshop, resist the urge to jump straight into brainstorming solutions. Instead, encourage your participants to really explore the problem at hand. Use techniques like "5 Whys" or "Root Cause Analysis" to get to the heart of the issue. By doing this, you'll be able to uncover any underlying issues that may have been missed in a traditional face-to-face setting.

For example, let us say your team is trying to figure out why customer satisfaction has been declining. Rather than jumping straight to ideas for improving customer service, spend some time really understanding the reasons behind the decline. Is it due to changes in customer behavior or expectations? Poor communication between departments? Once you have fully explored the problem, you'll be much better equipped to develop a solution that addresses the root cause.

Remember: taking extra time – particularly in virtual workshops - to discuss the problem might not sound like the most exciting thing in the world, but it is a crucial step in the problem-solving process. So, flip the focus and spend some extra time discussing the problem - your participants (and your solutions) will thank you for it.

Hack #20: Spend a lot more time discussing the problem than the solution.

#21 - Your Role: Stay Neutral

Mind your Mindset as Facilitator: Embracing Positive Neutrality for Impactful Results

As a facilitator, your mindset is the key to success. You need to be positive, neutral, flexible, outcome-driven, see the big picture, and stay focused, all at the same time. It is like being a ninja of facilitation, using your skills and expertise to guide a group towards a successful outcome.

The benefits: Mastering the art of positive neutrality helps you create a safe and inclusive environment where participants feel heard and valued. It allows you to remain impartial, objective, and non-judgmental, even in the face of challenging situations. By focusing on the big picture and the desired outcomes, you can help the group stay on track and achieve their goals.

Examples: Imagine you are facilitating a brainstorming session where one team member keeps shooting down everyone else's ideas. You need to remain neutral and positive, redirecting the conversation back to the objective and encouraging the team to build on each other's ideas. Or, perhaps you are facilitating a team-building workshop where some participants are more engaged than others. Your role is to remain flexible and focused, adapting your approach to meet the needs of the group and ensure everyone feels included.

Hack #21: Your mindset makes the difference: be positive, neutral, flexible, drive outcome, see the big picture and stay focused.

#22 - Timer

Race Against Time: How a Simple Timer Can Make or Break Your Next Facilitation Gig.

Time is the most precious commodity in the business world, and in facilitation, it is no different. One of the simplest yet most effective hacks to level up your facilitation game is to use a timer or timed exercises during your workshops, meetings, or training sessions.

By setting time limits for activities or discussions, you create a sense of urgency and focus among participants. It helps them stay on track and accomplish their objectives within the given time limit. Moreover, a timer can add excitement to an otherwise mundane task, making it a competition against time, which can improve engagement and motivation levels.

For example, in a brainstorming session, you can set a timer for 5 minutes for each participant to share their ideas. This encourages all participants to actively participate and prevents one or two dominant voices from taking over the conversation. In virtual settings, you can use the Microsoft Windows built-in timer or an online timer tool and share your screen to ensure everyone is aware of the time remaining during a break or for a task or activity.

Or you search for timers on YouTube: there are plenty of versions with preset time and variations of music. Create a bookmark list of YouTube timer videos for every duration and every mood you need them for.

Using a timer or timed exercises can help you achieve your workshop or meeting objectives within the allotted time limit. It also keeps participants engaged and focused, creating a sense of urgency and accountability. Ultimately, this hack can lead to more productive and effective workshops, meetings, or training sessions, and can help you stand out as a facilitator who delivers results.

Hack #22: Use a timer in virtual environments to clearly indicate how much time is left during a break or an exercise.

#23 - Accomplishments

From Bored to Brilliant: Empower Participants with a Sense of Accomplishment.

Nothing is more frustrating than attending a workshop and feeling like you have wasted your time. As a facilitator, your job is to ensure that every participant leaves feeling like they have accomplished something. How can you do that? Simple - make sure that each person has a clear understanding of what they have achieved during the workshop.

One way to do this is by setting specific goals for the workshop and ensuring that each participant is aware of what those goals are. You can do this by starting the workshop with a clear agenda and communicating the goals of each activity. At the end of each activity, take a few minutes to reflect on what was accomplished and how it contributed to the overall goal.

Another way to ensure that participants leave feeling accomplished is by providing opportunities for feedback and reflection. This can be done through group discussions, individual reflections, or feedback forms. Encourage participants to share their thoughts and feelings about the workshop and use their feedback to improve future sessions.

The benefit of this hack is that it helps to create a sense of accomplishment and satisfaction among participants. When people feel like they have achieved something, they are more likely to be engaged and motivated to continue learning and growing. Additionally, satisfied participants are more likely to spread the word about your workshop and encourage others to attend.

Hack #23: Ensure everyone leaves the workshop feeling they accomplished something.

#24 - Logistics

Logistics First, Dreams Second: The Prep Call You're Probably Ignoring.

You have done it. You landed the big gig. The workshop of your dreams is finally in your grasp. But before you get too lost in your head about all the amazing outcomes you are going to deliver, take a step back and think about something else: logistics.

Yes, logistics. That boring, practical stuff that seems like it should just work itself out. But trust us, it will not. And nothing will derail a workshop faster than realizing you forgot to order lunch or did not confirm the right address.

So, here is the hack: don't forget to focus on logistics during your preparatory phone call with the client. And we are not just talking about a cursory "oh yeah, we'll need some chairs" mention. We mean really go through everything with a fine-toothed comb: What's the start and end time, how many participants are there, which languages, what time zones are involved, will some teams meet onsite, are there technical restrictions, can everyone access the tools you like to use, etc.

The benefit? Well, besides avoiding those oh-so-embarrassing "sorry, we cannot access your whiteboard" moments, a thorough logistics check sets the stage for a smooth and professional workshop. It shows your client that you are on top of things, and it gives you peace of mind that you are not going to be caught off guard by any surprises.

And hey, if you are still not convinced that logistics matter, just think about the last time you attended a workshop where the connection was spotty or important documents could not be shared.

Hack #24: Never forget to check the logistics. In as much detail as possible.

#25 - Your Job: Not The Idea Generator

Facilitate, Don't Dictate: Let Participants Be the Idea Generators!

Stop being an idea generator! Your job as a facilitator is to guide the group towards their goals, not to come up with all the answers yourself. Let the participants do the heavy lifting and generate their own ideas. Your role is to support, challenge, and facilitate their creativity, not to impose your own.

The benefits of this hack are twofold: first, it empowers participants to take ownership of their ideas, leading to more engaged and invested group members. Second, it takes the pressure off you as a facilitator, allowing you to focus on guiding the discussion and keeping everyone on track.

For example, if you are leading a brainstorming session for a marketing team, instead of suggesting ideas yourself, encourage everyone to share their own thoughts and build on each other's contributions. Use prompts like "yes, and..." or "what if we..." to help the group expand on ideas and explore new directions. By the end of the session, the team will have a wealth of ideas they have generated themselves, and you will have facilitated a productive and collaborative discussion.

See yourself as a midwife. You help deliver the baby. But you were neither pregnant, nor in labor, nor do you have to worry about raising the child afterwards. You are just a midwife.

Hack #25: Your mindset makes the difference: be positive, neutral, flexible, drive outcome, see the big picture and stay focused.

#26 - Keep Cool

The Power of Positivity: Keep Your Cool When Things Go Wrong.

When facilitating a workshop, things may not always go as planned. Technical difficulties, unexpected interruptions, or difficult participants can throw a wrench into your carefully crafted agenda. However, no matter what happens, it is essential to stay positive and not let the group feel any negative emotions you may be experiencing.

Benefits: Staying positive in the face of adversity sets the tone for the entire group. If you become flustered or frustrated, it is likely that the participants will pick up on your negative energy and become disengaged. On the other hand, if you remain calm and positive, the group will feel more relaxed and confident, and they will be more likely to engage in the activities and discussions.

Examples: Let us say you're leading a virtual workshop, and the internet connection suddenly drops. Rather than panicking or getting angry, take a deep breath and calmly reassure the participants that you're working to resolve the issue. If a participant becomes disruptive or argumentative, don't take it personally or get defensive. Instead, try to understand their perspective and redirect the conversation back to the topic at hand.

Remember, as the facilitator, you set the tone for the entire workshop. By staying positive and maintaining a can-do attitude, you will help create a productive and enjoyable experience for everyone involved.

Hack #26: Stay positive, even if you have to fake it.

#27 - Activate Introverts

Crack the Code to Unleashing Introvert Power.

Are you tired of leading workshops where the same extroverted individuals dominate the conversation, while the introverts remain silent and disengaged? It is time to level the playing field and harness the untapped potential of your introverted participants!

One of the most crucial facilitation hacks to achieve this is by actively involving introverts right from the start. You have to break down the barriers and draw them out of their shell in the opening minutes of the workshop. By doing so, you create a safe and welcoming environment that encourages them to contribute and share their valuable insights.

To apply this hack, try using icebreakers that specifically cater to introverts. For instance, pair them up with a partner and ask them to share a personal story. This not only encourages them to speak but also helps to build trust and connections with other participants.

Another way is to use interactive tools such as post-it notes or digital whiteboards that allow introverts to contribute anonymously. This way, they can express their ideas and opinions without feeling judged or intimidated.

Remember, introverts are not shy or uninterested; they just need a little extra nudge to participate fully. By actively involving them from the beginning, you set the tone for an inclusive and productive workshop that values every participant's input. So, do not let the power of introverts go untapped - crack the code and unleash their potential today!

Hack #27: Break the ice for the introverts.

#28 - Body Language

Unleash the Power of Your Body Language.

Although virtual events have become the new norm, and we are all struggling to keep our audience engaged through a screen. But here's a secret - your body language can make all the difference! Yes, you heard it right. Even in the virtual world, your body language plays a crucial role in how you come across to your audience.

So, what can you do to make your body language work for you in virtual events? First, stand up when you want to convey a sense of energy and control. It is a simple trick that can make you appear more confident and assertive. And when you want to create a more relaxed atmosphere or be on the same level as your participants, sit down. This will help you connect with them on a deeper level and build rapport.

Another key aspect of body language in virtual events is using your hands to communicate. Make sure they are visible to the camera so that your audience can see your gestures. This will make you appear more expressive, engaging, and enthusiastic.

By incorporating body language into your virtual events, you can create a more engaging, memorable, and impactful experience for your participants. You will appear more confident, connect with your audience on a deeper level, and convey your message more effectively. As a result, you will be able to achieve your goals more efficiently and leave a lasting impression on your audience.

Hack #28: Use body language in virtual workshops to create specific moods.

37

#29 - Demos

Demo or Die: Why Showing is the Key to Successful Facilitation.

Are you tired of leading workshops where only a few participants seem to "get it" while others struggle to keep up? Do you want to ensure that everyone in your virtual breakout sessions understands the exercises you have planned? Then it is time to embrace the power of the demo!

Here is the deal: simply explaining an exercise verbally isn't always enough to help everyone understand what they're supposed to do. People have different learning styles, and some need to see something in action before they can really grasp it. That is why it's crucial to always accompany your explanations with a short demo, especially in the virtual world where there's more room for misinterpretation.

By showing exactly what you mean, you will save time and frustration in the long run. Participants will not waste time floundering, and you won't have to spend precious minutes re-explaining things. Plus, demos can be fun and engaging, adding a dynamic element to your workshops that can keep everyone interested and energized.

For example, let us say you're leading a virtual breakout session where participants need to brainstorm ideas for a new product. Instead of just telling them to "get creative," demonstrate the kind of thinking you are looking for by throwing out a few off-the-wall ideas yourself. Guide them to the virtual whiteboard where they should create the sticky notes.

Explain step by step how to get there and create a few notes by yourself in this demo. Hover over the text description of this exercise which you prepared on the board as well. Only then send them to the breakout sessions.

Hack #29: Demo your exercises, do not only explain them.

#30 - Think About The Clothes You Wear

Dress to Impress (Particularly from the Waist Up!)

The longer people work from home, the less they care about the clothes they wear. But please be aware that your attire can make a significant impact on how your participants perceive you and your workshop. The last thing you want is to look like a washed-up couch potato who rolled out of bed five minutes before the session.

So, before you jump on that video call, take a moment to think about what you are wearing. Consider the colors that complement your skin tone and make you look fresh and alert. Think about the formality of your clothes and whether they are appropriate for the team and the purpose of the workshop.

By dressing consciously, you show your participants that you respect them and the time they have invested in the session. It also helps to establish your credibility and authority as a facilitator. Plus, it sets the tone for a professional and productive session.

For example, if you are facilitating a creative brainstorming session, you might opt for a bright, colorful shirt to inspire your participants. On the other hand, if you are leading a more serious discussion on a sensitive topic, a muted, subdued outfit might be more appropriate.

Remember, the camera only shows what is from the waist up, so focus on making a great impression with your top half. With this simple hack, you will be surprised at how much of a difference a little attention to your wardrobe can make!

Hack #30: Make sure you are dressed appropriately.

#31 - Co-Facilitation

The Dynamic Duo: Why Co-Facilitation is the Ultimate Hack.

Facilitation is a demanding gig that requires a lot of energy, creativity, and expertise. But what if you could double your resources, brainpower, and charm? By teaming up with a co-facilitator, you can elevate your workshop from "meh" to "wow" in no time.

Firstly, it allows you to share the workload, meaning you can divide and conquer tasks like icebreakers, energizers, and group activities. Secondly, having a co-facilitator means you can play off each other's strengths, bringing different perspectives and skill sets to the table. Thirdly, co-facilitation creates a more dynamic and engaging environment for participants, as they get to experience different facilitation styles and personalities. Here are a few scenarios where co-facilitation could be a game-changer:

You are leading a team-building workshop for a group of thirty employees. By bringing in a co-facilitator from HR, you can provide additional expertise on topics like conflict resolution, diversity, and inclusion.

You are running a brainstorming session with a group of executives. By partnering with a co-facilitator from the design team, you can bring in fresh perspectives on creativity and innovation, as well as provide hands-on activities that spark the imagination.

You are leading a training session on project management for a group of junior employees. By involving a co-facilitator from the senior management team, you can provide guidance and mentorship, as well as create opportunities for networking and career development.

Co-facilitation is not just for big workshops or events. Even small groups can benefit from having two facilitators. So, do not be afraid to team up and become the dynamic duo that your participants deserve!

Hack #31: Use a co facilitator.

#32 - More Of That Chat

Chat it Out!

Forget about raising hands and taking turns - let us face it, group discussions can be awkward and time-consuming. That is why savvy facilitators turn to the chat function to keep the conversation flowing.

The benefits of using the chat function are numerous: It allows for real-time collaboration, where participants can quickly share their thoughts and insights without interrupting the speaker.

It creates an inclusive environment where everyone has a voice, not just the loudest or most confident participants. It captures valuable feedback and insights that can be referred to later, ensuring that no brilliant idea goes to waste.

To make the most of this hack, be sure to clearly explain how to use the chat function at the start of the workshop or meeting. Encourage participants to share their thoughts and questions throughout the session and be sure to acknowledge and respond to each message as appropriate.

Example: Imagine you are leading a brainstorming session and one participant comes up with a brilliant idea. Instead of interrupting the flow of the conversation, they can simply type their idea into the chat, and everyone can see it in real-time. This not only saves time, but it also ensures that everyone in the group has the opportunity to build on the idea and take it to the next level.

So, the next time you are leading a meeting or workshop, do not be afraid to "chat it out" - your participants will thank you for it.

Hack #32: Use the chat as often as possible.

#33 - Presentation Modes And Camera Perspectives

Visual Variety: The Secret to Engaging Workshops.

Do you know that feeling when you are sitting in a workshop and the presenter has been droning on in the same presentation mode for what feels like an eternity? Yes, we have all been there. That is why this hack is crucial to keeping your audience engaged and attentive.

By varying the presentation modes and camera perspectives, you keep your audience on their toes and give them something interesting to look at. Use the spotlight function to highlight different participants' faces throughout the workshop, so they feel seen and heard. If you are showing slides, do not be afraid to toggle the presentation on and off to encourage discussion amongst the team.

The benefits of this hack are twofold: not only does it break up the monotony of the workshop, but it also helps to keep your participants engaged and attentive. When people are stimulated visually, they are more likely to retain information and actively participate in discussions.

For example, let us say you are leading a virtual training session on conflict resolution. During a role-playing exercise, you could use the spotlight function to focus on each participant as they take turns acting out different conflict scenarios. This keeps everyone engaged and attentive, and also helps build empathy and understanding amongst the team.

In conclusion, do not settle for boring presentation modes. Keep your audience engaged and attentive by switching up the visual stimulation with this hack.

Hack #33: Get creative with camera perspectives and switch presenter modes frequently.

#34 - Tool Skills

Do not be a Fool, Master Your Tool.

It is time to face the harsh truth: if you can't handle your tools properly, you're just another amateur. As a facilitator, your tools are your weapons, and you need to master them to win the war.

In today's virtual world, this is more important than ever. Whether it is a virtual whiteboard, a video conferencing tool, or any other online platform, you need to know the ins and outs of your tools. Learning the shortcuts, hidden features, and time-saving tricks can make all the difference in your workshop.

Think about it - how impressed will your audience be if you effortlessly switch between screens, annotate a slide with ease, or create an engaging virtual brainstorm in seconds?

On the other hand, nothing is more frustrating than a facilitator who fumbles with their tools and wastes everyone's time. Do not be that facilitator.

Invest the time to master your tools and watch your professional impression soar. Plus, with the abundance of resources online, there is no excuse not to learn.

So, go ahead and watch those YouTube tutorials, practice until you are a pro, and show your audience who's boss. Remember, in the world of facilitation, the tools make the facilitator.

Hack #34: Master your tools.

#35 - Copy Notes, Don't Move Them

Do not Let Your Virtual Whiteboard Turn into a Sticky Note Graveyard.

Are you tired of ending up with a mess on your virtual whiteboard at the end of the workshop? You prepared a great structure and flow, but when the workshop is done, everything but the last section looks crippled? Do you want to avoid the nightmare of trying to recreate your workshop results later more or less from scratch? Then here is a hack that can save you hours of frustration: copy the sticky notes instead of moving them!

By copying instead of moving, you preserve the original structure and categorization of your content. This makes it easier for you and your team to refer back to the workshop results later and seamlessly integrate them into your documentation. Plus, it keeps your virtual whiteboard looking neat and organized, rather than a jumbled mess of misplaced sticky notes.

For example, let us say you are facilitating a brainstorming session with a team. They are generating lots of ideas and categorizing them into different buckets. Instead of moving the sticky notes to their respective groups, encourage them to copy the sticky notes and place the copies into the appropriate categories. This way, the original structure is preserved, and the team can easily refer back to their ideas in the future.

So, next time you are using a virtual whiteboard for your workshop, remember: copy, don't move! Your future self (the one after the workshop) will thank you.

Hack #35: Keep the structure of your interim results on virtual whiteboards by copying the sticky notes instead of moving them around.

#36 - Preparation

The Three Ps of Professionalism: Prepare, Prepare, Prepare!

You should not be one of those facilitators who thinks they can wing it online, just because you attended (or hosted) a zillion virtual meetings in the last couple of years. The virtual jungle is a whole different ball game, and it is not for the faint of heart. Good preparation is essential for success. And for the really important workshops you should better prep like your life (and your career) depends on it.

Why? Because unlike onsite facilitation, the virtual world is full of unpredictable technical glitches and distractions that can derail your workshop in a matter of seconds. Participants can "escape" your session with just one mouse click. Tools may not work as planned, either due to technical reasons or just because the participants will not manage them.

Without proper preparation, you will be left scrambling to fix things on the fly, and that's not a good look. So, what is the benefit of prepping like a pro? It gives you the confidence and flexibility to handle any situation that may arise. You'll be able to anticipate potential problems and have backup plans in place, making you a true master of your domain.

Preparation includes always having plan B (and perhaps even plan C and D). It includes becoming skillful on mastery level with the tools you use. It includes double checks and dry runs. In the virtual world, you need to be prepared for anything and everything. So, prep like your life depends on it, and watch your online workshops go from average to impressive.

Hack #36: Prepare. Prepare. And then: prepare again.

#37 - Managing Stakeholders

Do not Let Your Stakeholders Steal Your Show: Manage Them Like a Pro.

You are running your workshop but have the feeling that things do not turn out well. Some people clearly show that they do not enjoy your show and start making negative comments. And, worst of all, these people are your key stakeholders. They can make or break your workshop. So, here is the deal: you need to manage them like a boss, and you need to do it continuously.

When you manage your stakeholders effectively, you can ensure that your workshop stays on track and meets its goals. You'll also build trust with your stakeholders, which can lead to future opportunities. Additionally, you'll be able to address any concerns or objections before they become bigger issues.

Examples: Let's say you're leading a remote training session for a new software program. Your stakeholders include the IT team, the HR department, and the end-users. Before your workshop, you should have a conversation with each group to understand their needs and expectations. During the workshop, you should continuously check in with each stakeholder group to ensure that their needs are being met. For example, you might ask the end-users if the training is easy to understand and if they feel prepared to use the software after the workshop.

In another scenario, let's say you're leading a remote team-building session. Your stakeholders include the team members, the team leader, and the HR department. Before your workshop, you might have a call with the team leader to understand the team dynamics and any challenges they're facing. During the workshop, you might check in with the HR department to ensure that the session aligns with the company's culture and values. By managing your stakeholders continuously, you can create a workshop that meets everyone's needs and builds stronger relationships within the team.

Hack #37: Manage your stakeholders - continuously.

#38 - Clustering And Prioritization

From Chaos to Clarity: Prioritizing Ideas in the Virtual World.

Got a ton of ideas but do not know how to turn them into meaningful results for the next steps? Do not worry, we have got you covered. Here is a hack that will help you focus on what really matters in the virtual world.

The problem with online collaboration tools like Mural or Miro is that the traditional method of clustering sticky notes will not work. It is hard to make sense of hundreds of ideas on a screen. But fear not, we have got a solution.

Instead of trying to tackle everything at once, break your team into smaller groups of 4-6 people. Have them discuss priorities and present their findings to the larger group. This way, you get a more focused and manageable list of ideas to work with.

It's you have narrowed down your options to less than ten, it's time to use "usual" voting approaches like sticky dots or raised hands to determine the final list of priorities. This makes the process much faster, more interactive, and more engaging for everyone involved.

With this hack, you can efficiently prioritize ideas and move forward with a clear plan of action. This hack works at any phase of the workshop, whether you deal with a list of problems or ideas for solutions - anytime you are confronted with a large volume of virtual sticky notes and need to get them ordered and processed.

Hack #38: Prioritize ideas using breakout groups.

#39 - Energy

Mind the Energy Flow: The Secret to Keeping Your Virtual Workshop Alive.

When it comes to remote workshops, the energy flow is everything. It is not just about the content or the presenters - it is about the vibe you create. That's why it's important to plan your agenda with the energy flow in mind.

Think about it this way: if you start your workshop on a low note, you risk losing your audience's attention from the get-go. So, instead of just creating a topics list based on content and availability, consider the energy level each topic or speaker brings to the table. For instance, if you have a "dry" or technical topic on the agenda, you can balance it out by incorporating interactive parts or high-engagement activities. This will help keep your audience engaged and energized throughout the workshop.

The benefit of this hack is that it helps you create a dynamic and engaging workshop experience that your audience will remember. By taking care of the energy flow, you create an environment where participants feel motivated and excited to participate. This, in turn, can lead to better retention of information and a more successful outcome for your workshop.

When you plan your agenda and note down the steps, keep an eye on the energy level of each of these steps. You may consider using "energy level points" for each activity, from 0 (makes people fall asleep) to 10 (makes people freak out). This can help you create a decent flow and avoid energy drains or overkill moments.

Hack #39: Manage the energy flow.

#40 - Stay In The Call

The After-Party: Why Staying in the Virtual Room is the Ultimate Hack for Engaging Introverts.

As we all experienced many times, the loudest voice in the (virtual) room can often dominate the conversation. This can make it difficult for introverts, who may need a little more time to process their thoughts before speaking up. That is where the after-party comes in.

By staying in the virtual workshop room after the session has officially ended, you create a safe and relaxed environment where introverts can ask questions, share their thoughts, and engage in meaningful dialogue. This allows for a more inclusive and diverse conversation and ensures that everyone's voice is heard.

Not only does this hack benefit introverts, but it also benefits the overall success of the workshop. By creating a space for continued discussion, you can deepen the understanding and engagement of all participants, leading to more productive and impactful outcomes.

Example: Let's say you just finished a virtual workshop on a new project management software. During the workshop, one participant, Jane, seemed to be a bit quieter than the others. After the session officially ended, you asked if anyone had any questions or wanted to chat further. Jane, feeling more comfortable in a smaller group setting, asked a few questions and shared some of her concerns. This led to a more in-depth discussion about the software and its potential uses, which ultimately helped the group better understand how to implement it in their work. Without the after-party, Jane's valuable insights may have been missed.

Hack #40: Stay in the virtual workshop room after the session has ended.

#41 - Order Clarification

Avoid the Assumptions Trap.

Why not assume anything? Because it can make an "a*s" out of "u" and "me". Do not fall into this trap! Avoid assumptions and make sure that the expectations between you and your client are crystal clear. In remote workshops, it's more important than ever to be on the same page.

The benefits of this hack are numerous. Firstly, it ensures that everyone is on the same page, which reduces the likelihood of misunderstandings and conflicts. Secondly, it helps to establish trust between you and your client, as they will appreciate your attention to detail and your desire to clarify things. Finally, it makes your job easier, as you won't have to spend time dealing with misunderstandings or correcting mistakes that could have been avoided in the first place.

Let's say you're facilitating a remote training session on a new software tool for a group of employees at a company. You assume that everyone has access to the software and knows how to use it, so you jump right into the training without checking. However, halfway through the session, you realize that some participants are struggling to keep up because they do not have the software installed on their computers.

This could have been avoided if you had clarified the expectations with your client beforehand. By asking questions like "Do all participants have access to the software?" and "Do they know how to use it?" you could have avoided making assumptions and ensured that everyone was prepared for the training session.

In this case, the benefit of avoiding assumptions is that it helps to prevent confusion and frustration for both you and your participants. By taking the time to clarify expectations upfront, you can ensure that everyone is on the same page and that the training session runs smoothly.

Hack #41: No assumptions!

#42 - The Minutes Before You Begin

Start Strong: Activate Your Audience Before the Meeting Even Begins.

Do not let your online meetings fall flat before they even start! With the "Start Strong" hack, you can set the tone and engage your audience right from the get-go.

Take advantage of those crucial 3-5 minutes before the official start time to greet attendees by name, ask how they are doing, and get everyone feeling comfortable and excited to be there. This creates a welcoming environment and makes participants feel seen and heard from the very beginning.

Use simple equipment like portable speakers and a good microphone to play upbeat background music that energizes the room. And of course, have your camera on.

And when the meeting officially starts, start with a bang! Take a cue from radio or TV hosts and open with an attention-grabbing introduction that sets the stage for a productive, engaging session. No need to copy Robin Williams in "Good morning, Vietnam" – but a bit in this direction is how it works. You may even consider creating your very own "jingle" for each of your workshops, your signature music, background images, things people can see on your desk or behind your back, etc.

By starting strong, you'll be more likely to keep your audience engaged and invested in the content throughout the entire meeting.

Hack #42: Start before you start. And start strong.

#43 - Breaks

Get Your Participants Refreshed And Recharged With Timely Breaks.

As a facilitator, you want to ensure that your remote workshops are not only productive but also enjoyable. One of the easiest ways to achieve this is by incorporating timely breaks into your agenda. Research has shown that our attention span starts to wane after 45 minutes of concentrated effort, so it is important to give participants a chance to recharge.

The benefits of breaks are many. Firstly, they allow participants to step away from their screens and move around, reducing the risk of physical and mental fatigue. Secondly, they provide an opportunity for participants to network and chat with each other, which can foster a sense of community and belonging. Finally, they help to keep participants engaged and focused throughout the session.

So, how can you incorporate breaks into your remote workshops? Start by scheduling a short break of 5-10 minutes after every hour or two of the session. Use this time to encourage participants to stretch, grab a drink, or simply take a mental break. Avoid longer breaks, as they can cause participants to lose focus and make it difficult to regain momentum.

For example, if you are running a half-day workshop, you might schedule a 10-minute break after the first hour, followed by another 10-minute break after the second hour. This gives participants a chance to recharge their batteries and return to the session feeling refreshed and ready to learn.

Remember, breaks aren't just a nice-to-have - they're an essential component of any successful remote workshop. So, make sure to include them in your agenda and watch your participants stay engaged and energized throughout the session.

Hack #43: Plan enough (short) breaks.

#44 - Icebreakers

Keep Your Virtual Meetings on Fire with These Icebreaker.

Sure, we all know that icebreakers are great for getting things started and introducing people, but did you know they can also be used to revive a tired group after a long break or a low-energy section of a workshop?

Do not let the conversation stagnate and risk losing everyone's interest. Take a break and throw in a quick icebreaker to get everyone refocused and energized. Don't be afraid to get creative! Icebreakers can be anything from a fun group activity to a quick question or trivia game.

Ideally, you want to select icebreakers that will not only energize your team, but also reinforce the content that's been covered or is about to be covered. By doing so, you can help your team better understand and retain the information being discussed, while also building trust and fostering open communication.

But planning for icebreakers isn't just about matching them with the content – some icebreakers require additional materials, web sites, or other resources. That means you'll need to factor in time to gather and prepare these materials in advance.

For example, if you plan to use an icebreaker that involves a trivia game, you'll need to research and compile a list of relevant questions in advance. Or, if you plan to use an icebreaker that involves sharing photos or videos, you'll need to make sure everyone has the necessary technology and tools to participate.

So, if you're serious about using icebreakers to keep your virtual meetings on fire, be sure to plan and prepare accordingly. With a little bit of effort and creativity, you can turn a dull and unproductive meeting into a lively and engaging experience that benefits everyone involved.

Hack #44: Use icebreakers. And use them often.

#45 - Interact With Your Audience

Engage Your Virtual Participants: Diversify Your Interaction Methods.

You know from your own experience that it is not enough to simply present information to your audience if you want to create an outstanding workshop experience. To keep your audience engaged and actively participating, you need to use a variety of interaction methods. This means leveraging tools like mentimeter, Slido, and other polling and quizzing software. Additionally, chat functions can be a quick and easy way to encourage participation.

But be warned, simply using such methods for the sake of it is not enough. You need to have a purpose behind each tool you use. So, plan ahead and create relevant and interesting polls, quizzes, and icebreakers that serve a clear purpose.

Let's take an example: imagine you're leading a virtual training on effective communication skills with some focus on body language and facial expressions. A nice engagement method could be the icebreaker "two truths and a lie," before diving into the content. You could link this exercise to the question whether it is possible to detect liars via their facial expression or body language (spoiler alert: it isn't).

But if you did this same exercise in a strategy workshop before introducing the Osterwalder business model canvas, people would most likely be irritated and would ask themselves "what the hack was the purpose of this silly game?"

That is why it's essential to plan your activities in advance and test them out beforehand. Do not do them just for fun. Make sure they have a clear purpose and add value to the session, rather than being just a distraction.

Hack #45: Include a variety of interaction methods.

#46 - No Powerpoint

Do Not Use PowerPoint.

We know that this is not always possible, and sometimes a PowerPoint slide is the best way to illustrate a message.

But let us face it: Every time someone opens a PowerPoint presentation in a virtual meeting, all brains go into screen-saver mode. PowerPoint can be a real snooze-fest for participants. We are sure you recall countless virtual workshops where the facilitators just read off their slides, and you found yourself struggling to stay focused. And opened your inbox to answer some emails in parallel...

So, what is the alternative? Try using interactive tools that engage your audience. For example, you could use a virtual whiteboard to collaborate with your participants in real-time or use an online polling tool to get their opinions. You could also share short videos, images, or animations that capture your message more effectively than a boring slide deck.

The benefit of avoiding PowerPoint is that it forces you to be more creative and interactive in your approach. By engaging your participants in more unusual ways, you can make your session more memorable, more fun, and more effective. Plus, you'll avoid the dreaded death by PowerPoint.

For example, instead of showing a slide with bullet points, try using a virtual whiteboard to co-create a mind map with your participants. Or, instead of showing a list of dos and don'ts, share a short video or animation that demonstrates the concept in action.

In summary, ditching PowerPoint can be a game-changer for your virtual workshops. By using more engaging and interactive tools, you can create a more dynamic and memorable experience for your participants.

Hack #46: Do not use PowerPoint.

#47 - End On A High

The Last Impression Lasts. Make It Exceptional.

You know what they say about endings - they make or break the whole experience. So why do we often just peter out and let a virtual workshop come to a dull, uninspiring close? That is like going on a date and just awkwardly wandering off without a goodbye kiss - you are not leaving a lasting impression, honey!

Instead, take some inspiration from those radio and TV moderators who know how to wrap things up with a bang. End your remote meeting on a high note - make it memorable, inspiring, and leave your attendees feeling energized and ready to take action.

The benefit of this hack is twofold. First, it ensures that your meeting ends on a strong note, which will leave a positive impression on your attendees. Second, it sets the tone for future meetings, as attendees will be more likely to attend if they remember the wonderful experience they had.

So how do you end up on a high? Here is how you do it.

First you collect key takeaways, lessons learned, next steps or some feedback from the audience. Do this via chat, otherwise it will become boring and repetitive, and you risk that someone hijacks the moment.

Then you give the clear signal that the show is over now.

To make this impressive, just look at how TV moderators end a live show on stage. That is your blueprint. Raise your voice, thank the participants, and speak the prepared closing words. Tune in stimulating music and turn up the volume.

Wait till everyone has left the call. After a while you can lower the volume again. Now you are there for those people who wanted to connect with you after the end of the workshop.

Hack #47: End on a high.

#48 - Invite Critical People

Why Including Critics in Critical Workshops is a Smart Move.

You want to make sure your remote workshop goes smoothly and without any hiccups. That is why you may prefer to have only those people in the workshop that do not make trouble, who are easy-going or nice people.

But here is the thing: sometimes the people who can push back on your results are the very ones you should invite to the session. It may sound counterintuitive, but by including your critics, you are actually mitigating risk and ensuring that your findings are solid.

Think about it: if you are presenting a new strategy or project plan, you want to make sure that everyone is on board. By inviting the naysayers and skeptics, you can address their concerns head-on and get everyone on the same page. Plus, when you include those who may be critical of your ideas, you are showing that you're open to feedback and willing to listen to all perspectives.

Of course, you do not want to invite every single person who could potentially disagree with your findings. But by carefully considering who to invite, you can ensure that your workshop is inclusive and productive.

So do not be afraid to invite the uninvited. They might just be the key to a successful remote workshop.

Hack #48: Invite your critics.

#49 - Parking Lot

Do not Let Brilliant Ideas Slip Away: Create a Virtual Parking Lot!

In any remote workshop or training session, it's essential to keep participants engaged and focused. But sometimes, people can get carried away with their ideas, opinions, and questions, and it can be tough to stay on track. That's where a virtual "parking lot" comes in handy.

Think of it as a digital corkboard where you can pin all the ideas, suggestions, and questions that come up during the session. By doing this, you're letting the participants know that their input is valued and that their ideas won't be forgotten. At the same time, you're keeping the conversation flowing and avoiding getting sidetracked.

The benefits of using a virtual parking lot are many. First, it allows you to capture all the ideas and questions that arise during the session, without interrupting the flow. You can then review them at the end and address any outstanding issues. Second, it encourages participation and engagement from all participants, including those who may be hesitant to speak up during the session. Third, it can help you stay on track and avoid going down rabbit holes that can derail the session.

To create a virtual parking lot, you can use a shared document or a dedicated tool like Mural, Miro, MS Whiteboard or Lucidspark. Encourage participants to add their ideas and questions to the parking lot throughout the session, and make sure to revisit them occasionally. By doing so, you'll ensure that no brilliant ideas slip away and that everyone feels heard and valued.

Hack #49: Use a virtual "parking lot" to capture ideas and questions that can be addressed later.

#50 - Private Communication Channels

The Power of Secret Communication: Why Co-Facilitators and Key Stakeholders Need Their Own Channel.

When you are working with a co-facilitator or trying to keep a key stakeholder engaged, using a separate messaging channel can make all the difference.

Why is this hack so important? Well, imagine you are co-facilitating a workshop and your partner has an amazing point to make, but they are too shy to speak up in front of everyone.

With a secret communication channel, they can send you a message and you can seamlessly integrate their ideas into the discussion. Or let's say you're leading a virtual meeting with an important client, but they're distracted by their overflowing inbox. With a separate channel, you can gently nudge them back into the conversation without disrupting the flow of the meeting.

Of course, it's important to establish ground rules before using a secret communication channel. Make sure everyone involved knows how to use the channel and when it's appropriate to send messages. And, most importantly, be sure to keep an eye on the messages coming in so you don't miss any important contributions.

Hack #50: Use private communication channels to stay connected with co-facilitators and key stakeholders.

#51 - Sound Carpets For Silent Work

Silence is Golden: But A Sound Carpet With Ambience Music Can Be Your Diamond.

As a facilitator, you know that silence can be a powerful tool to promote reflection, discussion, and creativity. However, in a remote setting, it can also feel awkward and uncomfortable. To counteract this, consider playing soft background music during periods of silence to create a comfortable atmosphere that promotes relaxation and positive vibes.

By using a sound carpet with music during periods of silence, you can help your participants feel more at ease and create a more enjoyable and engaging workshop experience. The music can also help to prevent distractions from external noises or technical difficulties, which can be common in remote workshops.

Example: Imagine you're facilitating a remote team-building workshop, and you've just asked participants to take a few minutes to reflect on a particular question. Instead of letting the awkward silence take over, you play some soft instrumental music to create a relaxing atmosphere. Participants can use this time to think deeply and come up with thoughtful responses, without feeling uncomfortable or rushed.

Overall, incorporating a sound carpet with music is an easy and effective way to enhance your remote workshop and create a more enjoyable and engaging experience for your participants.

Hack #51: Use ambience music and sound carpets for silent work.

#52 - Shared Background Images

Virtual Background Power Play: Unleashing Team Spirit and Camaraderie.

In a remote setting, creating a sense of unity among participants can be challenging. But what if there was a way to instantly spark team spirit and collaboration? Enter the virtual background power play. By sharing a custom-made background image for all participants to set during the meeting or workshop, you can create a virtual team spirit that feels like you are all in the same room.

But wait, there is more! Take it up a notch by sharing different colored versions of the background and asking individuals to switch on a specific color. Voila! You have just created virtual sub-teams (team red, team green) that can collaborate and work together on group activities. Not only will this bring a fun and engaging element to your workshop, but it will also encourage participants to turn their cameras on and get involved in the session.

So, roll up your sleeves and get creative with those background images. Whether it is a picture of your team logo, a fun meme or a scenic landscape, the possibilities are endless. With a little preparation and some virtual background power play, you'll be well on your way to facilitating a remote workshop that's engaging, collaborative and unforgettable.

Hack #52: Share virtual background images.

#53 - Breakouts Secret 4: Clear Roles

Get rid of Embarrassing Moments in Breakout Session: The Power of Clear Roles.

Let us face it, breakout sessions can be a double-edged sword. On one hand, they provide the perfect opportunity for participants to share ideas, collaborate, and connect with each other. On the other hand, they can quickly turn into a chaotic mess if people are unsure about what they are supposed to do. This is where clear roles come in.

By assigning clear roles for breakout sessions, you are not only saving time but also increasing productivity and engagement. When people know what's expected of them, they're more likely to take action and contribute to the group. This leads to more meaningful conversations and a better overall experience for everyone involved.

For example, you can assign one person to be the timekeeper, another to be the note-taker, and a third to be the facilitator. The timekeeper ensures that the group stays on track, the note-taker captures key points and ideas, and the facilitator ensures that everyone has a chance to speak and that the conversation stays on topic.

So, the next time you're planning breakout sessions, make sure to give clear roles before you send the people off. It may seem like a small thing, but it can make a significant difference to the success of your event. Breakout like a boss and watch your participants thrive!

Hack #53: Give clear roles for breakout sessions.

#54 - Prefer Easy-To-Use Tools

Keep it Simple, Stupid.

Let us get one thing straight: nobody wants to sit through a virtual workshop that is more complicated than their taxes. As a facilitator, your job is to make the process as easy as possible for your participants. That means ditching the fancy tools and techniques and opting for simplicity instead.

Why is simplicity so important in remote settings? For one thing, attention spans are shorter than ever these days. If you are not engaging your participants right off the bat, you will lose them faster than you can say "Zoom fatigue." Plus, with so many distractions just a click away, you cannot afford to waste time on tools that are not intuitive.

The beauty of easy-to-use tools and methods is that they allow you to focus on what really matters: stimulating your participants' thinking processes, fostering collaboration, and encouraging communication. After all, that's what workshops are all about, right? You don't need a PhD to facilitate a remote workshop, and you shouldn't have to spend more than a few minutes explaining a tool.

If you need more than a few minutes to explain a tool or a method, they are useless.

So, every time you design an exercise, ask yourself: what's the simplest way to achieve the desired result? Whether it's a basic whiteboard, a shared Google Doc, or good old-fashioned pen and paper, stick with what works. Your participants will thank you for it.

Hack #54: Prefer easy-to-use tools and methods over sophisticated ones.

#55 - Harvest The Gems In The Chat

Do not Let Chat Gems Slip Away: Save, Paste & Amaze.

Tired of seeing your participants' brilliant ideas disappear into the chat void? Stop letting those chat gems slip away and start saving them for posterity! Regularly copy and paste chat responses into a text document during your virtual workshops, and then upload them to virtual whiteboards like Mural, Miro, or Lucidspark. Not only does this save your participants from the tedium of re-entering information they have already shared, but it also looks like pure magic to them when they see their ideas come to life in a visually stunning and organized way.

By capturing and organizing chat input, you can easily transform your virtual workshops into collaborative and productive sessions. You can use virtual whiteboards to create mind maps, group ideas, and facilitate brainstorming sessions. Plus, you can share the virtual whiteboard with your participants after the session, so they can see their ideas in action and have a tangible record of the session.

For example, imagine you are running a virtual brainstorming session to generate ideas for a new product launch. Participants are typing furiously into the chat, sharing everything from design concepts to feature requests. Instead of letting all of that information disappear into the chat ether, you capture it in a text document and then upload it to your virtual whiteboard like Mural. Once there, you use Mural's bulk-upload feature to quickly create a virtual whiteboard that organizes all of the ideas into different categories. The end result is a visually stunning and highly organized board that captures all of the participants' ideas in one place. When you share this board with the participants after the session, they're amazed by how their ideas have been brought to life, and they feel more invested in the project as a result.

Hack #55: Harvest your valuable chat content.

#56 - Impressive Virtual Whiteboards

Level Up Your Virtual Whiteboard Game.

Are you still using those boring, bland virtual whiteboards that make your participants yawn and zone out? Then it is time to level up. With Mural, Miro, Lucidspark & Co, you can create impressive, visually stunning virtual whiteboards that will leave your participants in awe.

Investing into your whiteboard's look and feel will not only make you come across more professional and credible, but it will also make your virtual workshops more engaging and enjoyable for your participants.

Imagine working on a virtual whiteboard that looks like a work of art, rather than a messy, amateurish one. Your participants will be more motivated to contribute and collaborate when they are having fun with the tool.

Mural, Miro & Co's also allow you to add various media types, such as images, videos, and diagrams, to your whiteboard, making your presentations more interactive and exciting.

Do not settle for mediocre virtual whiteboards. Invest in your whiteboards and level up your game. Your participants will thank you for it, and you will see the difference it makes in your virtual workshops.

Hack #56: Invest in creating impressive virtual whiteboards.

#57 - Breakouts Secret 5: Clear Instructions

Do not Let Confusion Derail Your Workshop.

Have you ever been thrown into a breakout room and found yourself staring blankly at your screen, unsure of what to do next? Do not let this happen to your workshop participants! Providing precise and clear exercise descriptions for breakout sessions is crucial to keep your remote workshop running smoothly.

Do not make the mistake of underestimating the importance of breakout room instructions. Without them, participants can easily become confused and disoriented, leading to frustration, timing issues, and awkward results.

To avoid this, take the time to craft bulletproof exercise descriptions that leave no room for confusion. Be sure to include clear instructions, expectations, and timelines for each activity. Consider providing examples or visual aids to help participants fully understand the task at hand.

By taking this hack seriously, you'll ensure that your breakout sessions run seamlessly, and your participants will feel confident and empowered to contribute their best work. Don't let confusion derail your workshop - make breakout room clarity a top priority.

Hack #57: Provide perfectly precise and clear exercise descriptions for your breakout session.

#58 - Backup Solutions

Plan for the Worst, Facilitate the Best!

Technical difficulties are the bane of every facilitator's existence, especially when it comes to remote workshops. You cannot control the internet gods or your computer's mood, but you can control how you react to these pesky problems. And that is where having a backup plan and some backup solutions comes in handy.

The benefit of having backup solutions is simple: it keeps your workshop running smoothly and minimizes stress levels for both you and your participants. Imagine you're in the middle of a crucial exercise and suddenly, your internet decides to take a coffee break.

What do you do? Well, if you have a backup plan in place, you can quickly switch to a different tool or platform and keep the show going.

So, here is what you need to do. First, identify your most important tools for the workshop. For example, if you are conducting a brainstorming session, a whiteboard tool might be essential. Next, research and test alternative tools that can serve as backups in case of technical difficulties. And finally, test your backup plan before the workshop starts. This will reassure you that you're prepared and makes you feel more at ease.

Here are some further ideas of how backup solutions could look like: Encourage participants to have pen and paper nearby, so they can take notes and draw diagrams if needed. Have a mobile device on hand with a hotspot feature, so you can switch to your phone's connection in case your Wi-Fi goes down.

If you're using slides, make sure to have a printed copy of them just in case your computer decides to act up. Or ask participants to print them beforehand. Use the snapshot function on your computer screen or smartphone to capture important visuals, such as graphs or charts. In case of possible power outages, make sure to have a backup battery or an alternative power source for your computer.

Hack #58: Have a backup plan for technical issues.

#59 - Unreliable Participants

Do not Let Unreliable Participants Ruin Your Remote Workshop: A Plan to Keep Things Running Smoothly.

Unreliable participants can be a real headache during remote workshops. Latecomers, dropouts, and other disruptions can throw off the rhythm of the workshop and leave other participants feeling frustrated or disengaged. But do not let them ruin your workshop! With a little planning and some smart strategies, you can keep things running smoothly.

One of the biggest challenges is dealing with latecomers. To avoid slowing everyone down, have a plan in place for how to catch them up. For example, you could assign them a partner who can bring them up to speed or provide them with a brief summary of what they missed during a break.

If you have too many or too few participants, be prepared to adjust your activities. Have a plan B in place beforehand or every breakout exercise, so you can quickly adapt and keep everyone engaged. For example, if you have too few participants for a group exercise, you could modify the activity to work in pairs or smaller groups.

Another common issue is when participants hop on and off the call, citing other important commitments. To avoid disruptions, clearly communicate your expectations in the beginning. Let everyone know that it's important to stay present and engaged during the workshop and plan your exercises so that they won't be disrupted by participants leaving early or joining late.

The key to managing all these issues is to plan accordingly. It WILL happen that people come late, and it WILL happen that the number of participants will change during the session. So be prepared, be flexible, and keep things moving forward!

Hack #59: Have a backup plan for unreliable participants.

#60 - Master Mural Within Minutes

Break the Ice and Learn the Tool: Get Creative with Whiteboard Warm-ups.

Do not assume that all your participants are tech-savvy, just because they signed up for your virtual workshop. Some may struggle with the basics of your virtual whiteboard tool, which can derail your entire session. Sending out tutorials in advance does not really work (nobody will watch them), but don't worry, there's a fun and effective solution. Use warm-up exercises that incorporate the whiteboard tool to get everyone comfortable and confident with it. This approach will help people learn by doing, and provide a safe and engaging environment to practice in.

The benefit of this hack is that it saves you time and keeps your participants engaged right from the start. Instead of spending precious minutes explaining how to use the tool or losing people's attention while demonstrating it, you can break the ice and learn the tool simultaneously. By starting with an interactive activity, you set the tone for a dynamic session and ensure that everyone is on the same page.

Example: Let us say you're leading a workshop on design thinking, and you want to use a virtual whiteboard to facilitate brainstorming and ideation. You know that some of your participants may not be familiar with the tool, so you decide to start with a warm-up exercise. You ask everyone to introduce themselves visually, using the whiteboard. They can drag and drop images, create cards with their names and interests, and add some color and personality to their profiles. You provide some prompts and examples to inspire them and encourage them to explore the tool and experiment with its features. This exercise not only helps people learn the tool, but also fosters creativity, collaboration, and self-expression. Once everyone has completed their profiles, you can use them as a springboard for further discussion and collaboration.

Hack #60: Use warmup exercises to make participants familiar with your virtual whiteboard.

#61 - Microphone, Camera, And Lighting

Upgrade Your Tech Game: Why Your Microphone, Camera, and Lighting Matter More Than You Think.

Do not underestimate the power of investing in quality equipment. Upgrading your microphone, camera, and lighting can significantly enhance the professional image you project during virtual workshops, improving your effectiveness as a facilitator.

Think of it this way - you wouldn't show up to an in-person meeting with a messy appearance or a mumbling voice, right? The same principle applies to virtual meetings. Poor audio and video quality can be distracting and frustrating for participants, and it can reflect negatively on your credibility as a facilitator.

By investing in a high-quality microphone, camera, and lighting, you can improve the clarity and professionalism of your virtual presence. For example, a better microphone can eliminate background noise and ensure that your voice is clear and easy to understand. A better camera can provide a sharper and more visually pleasing image, while good lighting can make you look more engaging and approachable.

So, do not skimp on your equipment - upgrade your tech game and reap the rewards of a more professional and effective virtual presence.

Hack #61: Invest in a better microphone, camera, and lighting.

#62 - Check What's Behind You

Calm Background, Focused Mind: Why Your Workshop Needs a Soothing Backdrop.

You might think that your workshop participants can easily focus on your presentation, but in a remote setting, distractions abound. One of the easiest ways to create a focused atmosphere is by providing a calm and soothing background for your presentation.

By using a simple image or solid color as your backdrop, you will help your participants avoid distractions and stay engaged with your content. Plus, it will be easier for you to share slides or other visuals without the background causing any visual noise.

For example, you could use an image of a serene nature scene, like a mountain range or a tranquil lake, to provide a calming atmosphere. Or you could use a solid color, like light blue or green, to evoke a sense of peace and serenity.

There are pros and cons to using a real or artificial background. Real backgrounds provide authenticity and visual interest but also pose the risk of distractions and privacy issues, while artificial backgrounds offer complete control and eliminate distractions but can feel inauthentic.

Blurred background effects can be a good compromise, reducing distractions and maintaining privacy while retaining some authenticity, but can also be inconsistent and prone to technical difficulties. Ultimately, the choice of background comes down to personal preference and the needs of the workshop situation.

Hack #62: Make sure you have a calm background.

#63 - Augment Your Virtual Reality

Elevate Your Virtual Experience with Tangible 3D Enhancements.

Are you tired of the same old virtual workshop format that leaves participants feeling disconnected and uninspired? Well, we have a hack that will take your remote workshops to the next level by incorporating tangible 3D elements into the mix.

By sending physical objects to your participants ahead of time, you can create a more immersive experience that extends beyond the digital realm. For example, in an exercise about decision making, called "Decision Poker", you could send a deck of cards for this exercise to each participant and use the cards later in the workshop. This adds a fun element of surprise, and it is another way of having people turn their cameras on, as they must show the cards they chose for each round to the camera.

But why stop at cards? Encourage participants to bring their favorite coffee mug or glass of wine to the virtual happy hour or send them a small gift that ties into the theme of the workshop. By incorporating physical objects, you'll create a more engaging experience that will keep participants excited and connected throughout the workshop.

The benefit of this hack is two-fold: not only does it enhance the virtual experience, but it also helps build stronger connections among participants. By sharing physical objects, participants can get a glimpse into each other's workspaces and personal lives, which can lead to more meaningful conversations and collaborations.

So, next time you plan a remote workshop, think outside the digital box and incorporate tangible 3D elements to elevate the experience for all participants.

Hack #63: Augment the virtual reality to the desks of your participants.

#64 - Idea Generation

How To Generate Many Ideas. And Then Even More.

Nobel prize winner Linus Paulin once said: "If you want to have a good idea, have many ideas". Easy said - but how do you do this effectively in a virtual environment? The key to success here is: strictly separate the divergent thinking (idea generation) from the convergent thinking (idea consolidation) stages. Well, this holds true also in the "real" world, not only in virtual settings. But the likelihood of distractions is much bigger when you are sitting in front of a computer. And the quality of ideation can be negatively impacted by this.

To implement this hack, set clear expectations for each stage and use technology tools such as digital whiteboards or brainstorming software to capture ideas.

In the virtual world it is even more important than in physical meetings to time-box ideation activities. Set specific time limits for ideation activities to keep participants focused and motivated. This will also encourage them to think quickly and creatively under pressure.

Something we found very productive is to utilize unconventional techniques to inspire creativity and encourage unconventional thinking. For example, you can have participants use paper and pencil to draw their ideas instead of typing them (see also hack #74 "Paper and pencil revisited"). You can also have them take a picture of their drawings and share them with the group.

When it comes to convergent thinking (the prioritization) we found it super powerful to make use of breakout rooms and smaller teams. You can find more about this in Hack #38 "Clustering and prioritization").

Hack #64: Strictly separate divergent and convergent thinking.

#65 - How To Share Links

Hold Their Hands Before Letting Them Click Away.

This looks like a simple hack, yet it is super powerful. Or the other way round: it helps prevent a stupid, unforced error.

We all know how easily distracted we can get when we are in a virtual meeting. One minute you are fully engaged, and the next thing you know, you have got 10 tabs open and have no idea what's going on in the meeting. Don't let your participants fall into this trap!

Before sharing any links to external tools or resources, make sure you explain the purpose of the link and give a quick demo of what they can expect to see. This ensures that everyone is on the same page and prevents them from getting lost in the internet rabbit hole. And then you share the link. If you share it before, people will just click on it, stop listening and start getting confused by the information they are confronted with.

For example, let us say you are facilitating a training session on a new project management tool. Instead of just sharing the link in the chat, say something like, "Okay, everyone, before we move on, let me quickly show you what you'll see when you click on this link. It will take you to a demo of the tool we'll be using, and you can follow along as I walk you through it."

By doing this, you're keeping everyone focused and engaged, while also making sure they understand the purpose of the link. So, the next time you're tempted to share a link without any explanation, remember to hold their hands before letting them click away!

Hack #65: Don't share a link before you explain what will happen when people click on it.

#66 - Use Sound Effects

Elevate Your Virtual Workshop with Funny Sound Clips.

Inject some fun and energy into your remote workshop by incorporating sound clips that create a positive atmosphere. Virtual meetings can sometimes feel dull and monotonous, especially when attendees are staring at a screen for hours on end. Adding sound effects such as clapping, laughing, cheering, and even cartoon sound bites can break up the monotony and bring a smile to your participants' faces.

Using funny sound clips can serve as a tool to engage your audience and keep them motivated throughout the session. For example, you can play a "Ta-Da" sound effect when someone successfully completes a task or share a "Womp womp" sound to lighten the mood when someone makes a mistake. These sound effects can be used to encourage participation, emphasize key points, and build a sense of community among participants.

While some virtual collaboration tools provide built-in sound clips, their range is often limited. However, by using an external speaker and creating your own playlist of sound effects, you have the flexibility to curate the sounds that best suit your workshop's purpose and tone. At the end of our book, you'll find a QR code which leads you to a web page with useful stuff such as pre-made playlists of sound clips that you can use right away.

Hack #66: Use sound effects.

#67 - Avoid Hybrid Events

Virtual or Bust: Why Hybrid Workshops Could be Holding You Back.

When faced with the challenge of having some participants meet onsite while others join virtually, the solution is simple: make the entire workshop virtual.

While it may seem like a good compromise to have some participants meet in person, it creates an unfair advantage for those who are physically present, leading to a potential divide between the two groups. By keeping everyone in the same virtual environment, you create a level playing field for all participants, allowing everyone to contribute and collaborate equally.

This hack ensures that all participants have equal opportunities to engage and contribute to the workshop, regardless of their location. It creates a sense of unity and fosters collaboration, as all participants are working towards a common goal.

By avoiding the divide between onsite and virtual participants, you also ensure that everyone feels included and valued, ultimately leading to a more successful and productive workshop.

Example: Let us say you are leading a virtual workshop with 20 participants, but 5 of them are able to meet onsite in a single location. While it may seem like a good idea to have those 5 participants meet in person, it could potentially create a divide between the onsite and virtual participants.

Instead, opt for a fully virtual workshop to ensure that all participants have the same experience and opportunities to participate. Use virtual collaboration tools and breakout rooms to facilitate group discussions and activities, and make sure to provide clear instructions and guidelines to keep everyone on track. By doing so, you'll create a more cohesive and productive workshop for all participants.

Hack #67: Avoid hybrid events.

#68 - Running Hybrid Events

Hybrid Events Done Right: The Co-Facilitator Solution.

Although we said in our last hack that you should not run your sessions in a hybrid setup, sometimes you cannot avoid it. And these events can be a nightmare to facilitate. You have got people in the room, people on their laptops, and people on their phones. How do you keep everyone engaged and make sure no one gets left behind?

The solution: bring in a second moderator or co-facilitator to help manage the hybrid setup. This person must be with the onsite team, and the real magic happens when you position the onsite moderator just as a co-facilitator, rather than the main host. This sends a clear message that everyone in the room is on the same level as those joining remotely. It helps prevent any "us vs. them" dynamics from forming and ensures that everyone has an equal voice in the conversation.

For example, imagine you're facilitating a training session for a company with offices in different locations. Some participants are in the same room as you, while others are joining remotely. By bringing in a remote moderator, you can ensure that everyone feels included and engaged, regardless of their location.

So, if you want to ensure your next hybrid event is a success, don't go it alone. Bring in a moderator or co-facilitator to help manage the logistics and keep the energy high. And make sure to position the onsite facilitator as a co-facilitator to prevent any "we and they" dynamics from forming.

Hack #68: Never run hybrid sessions alone. Use a co-facilitator to manage the onsite team.

#69 - Treat Remote Participants Like VIPs

Do not Leave Your Remote Participants Hanging: The VIP Treatment Hack.

This hack is dedicated to situations where most people are in the same room, but you have one or just a few remote participants. Being one of those remotes can be a lonely and disconnected experience. They feel like an outsider, missing the dynamics and energy of being physically present with the rest of the group.

To prevent this, use the "VIP Treatment Hack". By providing each remote participant with a chair and a laptop or computer screen, you can create a virtual seat at the table for them. This not only helps them feel like a real participant, but also allows them to fully engage with the content and actively participate in the discussion. Plus, they can see the other participants in the room and feel more connected to the group. This kind of setup is often used on TV, e.g., when some participants of interview round or talk shows are dialed in (they only use larger screens).

Alternatively, you can project all external participants onto a big smart screen in the room, giving them a presence and visibility that is hard to achieve with a small laptop screen. This can help them feel more included in the group and participate as if they were there in person.

By implementing the VIP Treatment Hack, you show your remote participants that they are valued and essential members of the group. This can increase their motivation, engagement, and overall satisfaction with the session. So, don't leave your remote participants hanging - give them the VIP treatment they deserve!

Hack #69: Treat remote participants like VIPs in a talk show.

#70 - Using Whiteboards In Hybrid Sessions

Do not Be a Whiteboard Snob - Empower Your Hybrid Team to Collaborate Digitally.

When you are running a hybrid session with some people onsite and others remote, it is crucial to create a level playing field for everyone. That means ditching any physical whiteboard (onsite) and ensuring that everyone has access to the same digital workspace and virtual whiteboard.

By providing individual computers for all participants to work on, you can foster a sense of equality and collaboration, regardless of whether they're in the same room or on the other side of the world. Plus, this approach has some nifty benefits:

First off, it is more efficient. Instead of having people scribble their ideas on paper or sticky notes, you can capture everything in one central location that everyone can access and edit in real-time.

It is also more inclusive. People who may not feel comfortable speaking up in a group setting can contribute their ideas anonymously or through chat functions.

Finally, it is more environmentally friendly. You are not wasting paper, markers, or sticky notes that will just end up in the trash.

So, next time you are running a hybrid session, do not be a whiteboard snob. Give your team the tools they need to collaborate effectively, regardless of where they are.

Hack #70: Use virtual whiteboards also in hybrid sessions.

#71 - Using Breakouts In Hybrid Settings

Breakout Mixology: The Secret to More Engaging Hybrid Workshops.

When you plan breakout sessions in a hybrid setting, then do not fall into the trap of separating locals and remote attendees into separate breakout groups. Instead, create physical breakout rooms at your onsite location and mix the teams up. This hack is all about fostering a sense of inclusion and collaboration, regardless of physical location. By mixing onsite and remote participants in breakout sessions, you are encouraging diverse perspectives, building stronger relationships, and improving overall engagement.

The benefits of this hack are two-fold. First, it encourages more collaboration and idea-sharing between onsite and remote attendees, which can lead to better problem-solving and more creative solutions. Second, it helps to create a more inclusive environment, where remote attendees don't feel like they're missing out on the "real" workshop experience. By mixing the teams up, you're creating a more level playing field and fostering a sense of belonging for all participants.

Example: Let's say you're facilitating a workshop with 20 participants, 10 onsite and 10 remote and you would need two breakout groups for your exercise. You could split them up into one onsite group with 10 and one remote group with the other 10. A much better solution is to use two physical rooms onsite and send 5 of the local and 5 of the remote people into each. If you need 4 breakout rooms for your exercise, you should have 4 rooms onsite available and fill them with the same approach.

Hack #71: When using breakout rooms in hybrid settings, split up the locals into different rooms and mix them with the remote participants.

#72 - Breaking The Ice In Hybrid Settings

Bridging the Gap Between Onsite and Offsite Participants in Hybrid Workshops.

In hybrid settings, it is crucial to compensate for the "social cold start" by consciously planning the start of your workshop to ensure that onsite and offsite participants can get to know each other.

Imagine you are hosting a hybrid workshop where some participants are physically present while others are joining remotely. The onsite participants are already comfortable with each other - they've greeted each other with handshakes, shared a few laughs, and have established a sense of comradeship. Meanwhile, the offsite participants are left feeling like outsiders, unable to perceive the same level of social interaction as their onsite counterparts.

This is what we call the "social cold start," and it can make or break a hybrid workshop. To overcome this, a conscious effort must be made to bridge the gap between onsite and offsite participants.

One effective method is to have a "virtual coffee break" or "virtual speed dating" session where onsite and offsite participants are paired up to introduce themselves and get to know each other on a personal level. This way, they can establish a connection and build rapport before diving into the actual workshop.

Whatever icebreaker you use, you need to carefully plan this first activity to avoid the social cold start.

Hack #72: Carefully plan warmup activities in hybrid settings to avoid the social cold start.

#73 - Use Video Recordings Of Your Workshop

Show, Do Not Just Tell: Use Video Demos To Make Your Remote Workshops Feel Real.

During the topic clarification phase, many clients may struggle to imagine how a remote workshop will work, especially if they are used to physical workshops or have had poor experiences with virtual meetings. To help them better understand what they can expect, create video demos that highlight the tools and virtual whiteboards you will be using in action. By giving clients a preview of what the remote workshop will look and feel like, you can help them feel more confident and excited about the experience.

Using video demos to highlight your remote workshop tools and features can provide several benefits. First, it can help to alleviate any concerns or confusion that clients may have about how the workshop will work. Second, it can help to build trust and credibility with your clients by showing them that you have a clear plan and the expertise to execute it. Finally, it can help to create excitement and engagement around the workshop by giving clients a sneak peek into what they can expect.

Example: Let us say you are facilitating a virtual strategy development session for a group of clients. Before the workshop, you create a video demo that shows how you will use virtual whiteboards to develop the strategy, as well as how participants can use features like chat and breakout rooms to collaborate effectively. You send the video demo to clients ahead of time, along with a brief explanation of how the workshop will work. By doing so, you help to set expectations and build excitement for the workshop, while also giving clients a clear sense of what they can expect.

Hack #73: Show your clients what they will get using video demos.

#74 - Paper And Pencil Revisited

Why Going Old School with Paper and Pencil is the Secret to Successful Remote Facilitation.

Who said paper is dead? While advanced techie tools can be useful for virtual facilitation, sometimes you need to go back to basics to truly connect with your participants. By incorporating paper and pencil exercises into your virtual sessions, you can tap into different parts of your participants' brains, fostering creativity, focus, and engagement.

This approach has quite a few benefits: It boosts engagement: Incorporating physical materials into your virtual sessions adds a new dimension to your exercises and keeps participants engaged and focused. It stimulates creativity: Paper and pencil exercises can help to tap into different parts of participants' brains, leading to more creative solutions and ideas.

It improves memory retention: Writing things down on paper can help to reinforce information in the brain and aid memory retention. It is even inclusive: Not everyone is a tech wizard or has access to the latest devices. Using paper and pencil ensures that all participants can participate fully in your virtual sessions.

Example: In a virtual brainstorming session, rather than having participants type out their ideas in a shared document, have them write them down on paper first. In a second step they can "copy and paste" the best ideas into a chat or simply hold them up to the camera.

This allows everyone to see each other's ideas and fosters a sense of collaboration and community. You can also use paper and pencil for icebreakers, drawing exercises, or even simple notetaking during a presentation.

Hack #74: Use paper and pencil in remote workshops.

#75 - Overcome Language Barriers

Lost in Translation? Not With This Language Hack!

Language barriers can be a pain in the butt - but the virtual environment provides help with this much better than in any onsite situation.

To make this hack work, ensure you have the technology support in place. Encourage participants to use online translation tools such as Google Translate or DeepL and provide links and guidance on how to use them. Additionally, make use of the transcript functions available in many virtual platforms, which can provide live transcription in multiple languages.

But do not stop there - get creative with your language hacks! Consider using visuals or graphics to help illustrate key points, or even consider incorporating games or exercises that do not require a high level of language proficiency. By doing so, you will help level the playing field and ensure that everyone feels involved and engaged.

For example, if you are conducting a virtual team-building workshop with participants from different countries, you could use a virtual whiteboard tool to have everyone draw a picture of something that represents their culture, without any words. This way, everyone can participate regardless of language proficiency and learn about each other's backgrounds in a fun and interactive way.

By providing language hacks like these, you can make sure that language does not get in the way of a successful virtual workshop.

Hack #75: Be mindful about language barriers and use available tools and creative exercises formats to overcome this.

#76 - Use Animated Gifs

Gif Me Some Laughter: How Animated Gifs Can Add Humor To Your Virtual Workshop.

With the power of animated gifs, you can add some much-needed humor and personality to your chat interactions. Whether you want to react to a comment, express agreement, or disagreement, or simply lighten the mood, gifs can do it all.

The benefits of using gifs in your virtual workshop are endless. For one, they can break the ice and make your participants feel more comfortable in a remote setting. Gifs also provide a fun and engaging way to communicate, which can help prevent distractions and keep participants focused on the task at hand. Plus, using gifs shows that you are a savvy and creative facilitator who knows how to inject some personality into your workshops.

So how do you use gifs in your virtual workshop? Some platforms like Slack and Microsoft Teams have built-in gif features that you can use right away. If you need more variety, you can visit giphy.com, which has a massive collection of gifs that you can easily browse and download. Simply copy and paste the gif into the chat window and watch as your participants react with laughter and engagement.

For example, if someone makes a joke during the workshop, you can respond with a gif of a laughing baby or a dancing cat to show that you appreciate their humor. Or if you want to express agreement with a participant's comment, you can use a gif of a thumbs up or a high-five. The possibilities are endless, so do not be afraid to get creative and have fun with it!

Hack #76: Use animated Gifs.

#77 - Meet Your Client In Person

Get off Your Screen and Meet Them in Person!

Do not let the convenience of remote communication trick you into thinking it is the only way to connect with your clients. Meeting in person, even just once, can make a world of difference in establishing a strong and lasting relationship. It allows you to build trust, get a better sense of their needs and expectations, and create a more personal connection.

The benefits of meeting in person are especially important for remote facilitators, who may struggle to establish rapport and engagement with their clients. By taking the time to meet in person, you will be able to create a foundation of trust and understanding that will carry over into your virtual interactions.

Once you have met in person, you can continue to communicate remotely, but make sure to stay "visible" and maintain that personal connection. Use video recordings of your workshops to show clients that you are actively engaged and invested in their success, even when you are not physically in the same space.

For example, if you are facilitating a team-building workshop for a remote team, consider traveling to their location for the kickoff session. This will allow you to get to know the team members, understand their dynamics, and tailor your facilitation approach accordingly. After that initial in-person meeting, you can continue the rest of the sessions virtually, but you will have established a stronger connection with the team and set the stage for a successful workshop.

Hack #77: Meet your client in person. At least once.

#78 - Breakouts Secret 6: No Surprise Ending

Do not be a Breakout Room Dictator - Inform before you Interrupt.

Do you know that feeling when you are in the middle of a heated discussion with your colleagues, and someone abruptly pulls you out of the conversation? Do not be that person! As a remote facilitator, it is crucial to respect the time and energy participants invest in their breakout room conversations.

So, before you drop the bomb and drag them back to the main room, give them some heads up. At least 5 minutes, 1 minute, and 10 seconds before closing the breakout room, inform your participants. This way, they can wrap up their discussion, exchange contact details or share any last-minute thoughts.

We get it; you may feel tempted to stick to a fixed timer. However, a rigid time constraint can disrupt the flow of conversations or leave participants feeling cut-off. By giving them a heads up, you show that you value their contributions and time. Plus, it ensures a smooth transition back to the main room, keeping the energy high and preventing participants from feeling disoriented.

For example, you could say: "Hey, folks, you have five more minutes to wrap up your conversation. Please exchange your contact details or finalize your action plan. We'll be closing the breakout room in 5 minutes." Repeat the same message one minute before closing and a final 10-second warning.

In conclusion, avoid being a breakout room dictator and inform before you interrupt. Give participants ample time to complete their discussions, exchange contacts, and say goodbye before coming back to the main room. It is a small gesture that goes a long way in creating a respectful and inclusive virtual environment.

Hack #78: Inform the participants before you close the breakout rooms.

#79 - Lunch Together

Lunch is Not Just for Eating!

Eating alone at your desk is a sad sight. Why not spice up your remote workshop and make it a shared experience with a joint lunch break? It is time to stop being a lonely wolf and synchronize with your team for a virtual feast! With joint lunch breaks, you can bring your team closer together and build a stronger bond. You will be surprised at how much more relaxed and friendly your colleagues will be when they are chomping down on some delicious food. In hybrid sessions you may consider using a "Digital Hybrid Lunch" to include remote attendees in lunch as well.

Plus, this hack is great for productivity. Taking a break to eat and chat can recharge your batteries and give you the energy you need to power through the rest of the day. It is also an excellent opportunity to get to know your colleagues on a personal level, which can lead to more effective communication and collaboration in the long run.

To make this hack work, schedule a joint lunch break and share the link to a delivery service so that everyone can order their own meal. It is best if everyone is in the same time zone, and even better if they're in the same city. You can even spice things up by playing games or holding a fun trivia quiz during the meal. In the end, it is all about bringing people together, building relationships, and creating a positive remote work culture.

Hack #79: Have lunch together.

#80 - Document Your Progress

Snapshots and Screencaps: Your Virtual Workshop's Secret Weapon

Do not let your virtual whiteboard scribbles go to waste - snap them up! Just like in-person workshops, virtual workshops can benefit from having a visual record of the ideas and discussions that took place. Take screenshots and screencaps of your virtual whiteboards and collate them into a PPT or PDF document that you can share with your clients after the workshop. Not only does this serve as a helpful reminder of what was discussed, but it also showcases your facilitation skills and the value you bring to the table.

Think about it - your clients are investing time and money in these workshops, so why not give them something to show for it? Plus, having a visual representation of the ideas and insights that were generated during the workshop can help your clients take action and implement the learnings in a more meaningful way.

For example, let us say you're facilitating a virtual brainstorming session with a team. As the ideas start flowing, you capture them on the virtual whiteboard and take screenshots throughout the session. After the workshop, you compile the screenshots into a PPT and send it to the team. They are now able to see all the ideas in one place, which can spark further discussion and action.

And if you really want to go the extra mile, use screen recording tools to capture short video clips of the workshop. This can help recreate the atmosphere and energy of the workshop, which can be especially helpful if not everyone was able to attend.

Hack #80: Create your documentation while you do the workshop.

#81 - Ask The Audience

Turning Your Audience into Active Participants by Flipping Questions Back at Them.

Instead of always being the one answering the questions, try returning questions to your audience to increase interactivity and engagement.

As a facilitator, it is easy to fall into the trap of always being the one answering the questions. While this is the usual expectation of you as the expert or as the host, it can also create a one-sided dynamic where the audience feels like passive participants. By flipping the script and returning questions to your audience, you can create a more dynamic and engaging workshop experience.

By returning questions to your audience, you not only encourage active participation and engagement, but you also empower your audience to take ownership of the conversation. This can lead to deeper, more meaningful discussions and a greater sense of investment in the overall outcome of the workshop.

Example: Let us say you are leading a virtual workshop on marketing strategies. A participant asks, "What's the best social media platform for our business?" Instead of answering directly, you could respond with, "That's a great question. What social media platforms have you had the most success with in the past?" This not only gets the audience thinking but also opens the conversation for multiple perspectives and experiences.

As the likelihood of participants disengaging in a virtual event is much higher than in onsite settings, this old communication technique deserves a strong revival.

Hack #81: Engage your audience by returning questions to them.

#82 - Avoid Static Content

Mind the Average Human Attention Span!

Nobody wants to sit through a dull and boring presentation with static content. Research has proven that adults have an attention span of less than 10 seconds when faced with static content with voice-over. That is barely enough time to catch their attention! If the visual does not change in that time frame, your audience will start fidgeting, checking their phones or even worse, dozing off.

But fear not! There is a simple solution to this problem - ditch the static content altogether! Say goodbye to those dreary PowerPoint presentations and hello to a more engaging and interactive approach.

If you must use PDF documents, static PowerPoint, or any other non-animated content, try using animated visuals such as virtual laser pointers or maker pens to keep your audience engaged. Not only will this help to capture their attention, but it will also help to make your presentation more memorable. Your audience will appreciate the effort you put in to keep them engaged and they will leave your presentation feeling energized and motivated.

So, next time you are planning a virtual workshop, don't settle for static content. Use animated visuals to keep your audience engaged.

Hack #82: Do not use static content.

#83 - Allow Moments Of Silence

Embrace the Awkward: Why Silence is Golden in Remote Facilitation.

As a facilitator, it is natural to want to fill every moment of silence with chatter or questions to keep the conversation going. But when it comes to virtual workshops, introverts can easily get drowned out by more extroverted participants, leading to an unbalanced conversation. That is why it is important to stand the silence and let introverts take their time to process and respond.

Embracing silence in virtual facilitation allows introverts to feel more comfortable and included in the conversation, leading to more thoughtful and diverse contributions. By giving participants time to process, you also encourage more critical thinking and deeper discussions.

Example: Imagine you are leading a virtual brainstorming session with a group of colleagues. After posing a question, you notice that there is a long pause before anyone speaks up. Instead of rushing to fill the silence, you give everyone a moment to think before continuing the discussion. Eventually, one of the quieter members chimes in with a brilliant idea that sparks further conversation and leads to a breakthrough.

Anytime you feel tempted to fill the silence in a virtual workshop, take a breath and remember: sometimes, the best ideas come from those who take their time to think.

Hack #83: Allow moments of silence.

#84 - Watch Out For Signals Of Distraction

Eyes on the Prize: Keeping Your Audience Engaged in a Remote Workshop.

In a virtual workshop, it is easy for attendees to get distracted by their other work or online activities. But as a facilitator, it is crucial to keep your audience engaged to ensure the success of your workshop. One way to do this is to monitor their attention by paying attention to their eyes. If their gaze keeps wandering across the screen, it is a sign that they might be multitasking or checking their email.

Here is another cool hack to check their attendance, particularly in sessions where many people have their cameras on: if the faces of people suddenly light up, it is a sign that they've opened another window, possibly a web browser with a bright background that's catching their attention. If their faces turn dark, then they must have opened a window with a dark background. This flickering effect is easy to detect and tells you that the attention of the crowd is going down.

By being aware of these signals, you can take action to keep your audience focused and engaged. This might involve changing the pace of the workshop, adding interactive activities, or even taking a break to allow attendees to address any urgent matters.

But do not go too far. It is not realistic to expect everyone in the audience to stay 100% focused on you all the time. So, it is important to accept a certain level of distraction with your participants.

People believe they can multitask, even if they cannot. And if you are honest with yourself, you may realize that you also engage in some side activities during remote workshops and still manage to grasp the main points.

Hack #84: Observe your audience and watch out for the flickering effect.

#85 - Breakouts Secret 7: Give Them Enough Time

Breakout Blues: Why Your Quickie Breakouts are Killing Your Virtual Workshops.

Are you trying to cram too many activities into your virtual workshops? Do you rush through breakout sessions just to tick them off your agenda? Here is the truth: Quickie breakouts are killing your workshop's potential.

Instead of giving your participants a measly 5-minute break, aim for a minimum of 10 minutes for easy tasks, 30 minutes for discussions, and up to an hour if results need to be presented. This gives your participants enough time to digest the information, reflect on their thoughts, and recharge their batteries.

By giving ample time for breakouts, you are allowing participants to interact with each other, learn from different perspectives, and generate new ideas. This leads to more engaged participants, better collaboration, and more meaningful outcomes.

For instance, let us say you're facilitating a virtual brainstorming session. You divide your group into breakout rooms and give them 10 minutes to generate ideas. After the break, each group presents their top ideas, and the entire group discusses which ideas to pursue. By giving them enough time to collaborate and reflect, you are increasing the chances of producing creative and relevant ideas. Even if you time-box the idea generation to just 5 minutes, the teams still need to form and organize themselves, ensure they have understood the task correctly, agree on someone to present back - and all these activities take time. If you only provide them with the net time required for the exercise, they will feel rushed, leading to a decline in the quality of results.

So, do not be a breakout buzzkill. Give your participants the time they need to flourish and contribute to your workshop's success.

Hack #85: Give your teams enough time for their breakout sessions.

#86 - Debriefing After Exercises

Say Goodbye to the Round Robin Blues.

Many facilitators still use the "traditional" debriefing technique of having participants present back their findings in round robins also in virtual settings. The reason for this may be that they are alone in the main room while their participants are engaged in breakout sessions. This creates a perceived need for the facilitator to "break" the silence. However, this is a misconception as the teams have been active during that time.

Very often such debriefings after collaborative exercises or breakout sessions turn out to be dull and tedious. It is much more effective to take a birds-eye view of what has been discussed and provide a summary to your participants.

This hack can save you time and keep your virtual workshop engaging by allowing participants to add selected topics in a more targeted way. For example, you can ask specific questions like, "John, I noticed you contributed a great idea about xyz. Can you please share your thoughts on that with the larger team?"

By avoiding the round robin approach, you also prevent the risk of participants repeating what others have already said, which can be dull and counterproductive. Plus, by summarizing the main points of the exercise, you help everyone stay on the same page and ensure that no important findings or ideas are missed.

The reason so many facilitators still use the "traditional" debriefing technique in virtual settings may be that they are alone in the main room while their participants are engaged in breakout sessions. This creates a perceived need for the facilitator to "break" the silence. However, this is a misconception as the teams have been active during that time.

Hack #86: Avoid tedious round robin debriefing sessions after breakout exercises.

#87 - Keep Your Energy Level Up

Sweat, Don't Stress: Stay Energized During Breakouts with Quick Exercises.

As a remote facilitator, your energy level directly affects the quality of your workshop. It is important to keep yourself fresh and energized, especially during breakout sessions when you are not actively facilitating. But let us be real, checking email during these breaks is a trap that can quickly spiral into stress and distraction.

Instead, use these few precious moments to do some quick exercises that get your blood pumping and your mind focused. Keep some exercise equipment handy, like dumbbells, resistance bands, or a yoga mat, and do some squats, pushups, curls, or stretches. Just a minute or two of physical activity can help you clear your head and come back to the session with renewed energy.

Not only will this hack help you stay focused and engaged throughout the workshop, but it will also set a good example for your participants. When they see you prioritizing your physical well-being, they will be more likely to do the same. So do not stress, sweat it out and keep the energy flowing!

Hack #87: Stay energized during breakout sessions with quick physical exercises.

#88 - Check The Technology

Do not Be a Tech Wreck: Do a Thorough Tech Check Before Key Events.

No matter how experienced you are, technical issues can happen to anyone. This sounds like a no-brainer and something obvious, but reality shows that it's too often not taken seriously enough: it's crucial to do a thorough tech check before your important sessions to ensure a smooth and hassle-free experience for everyone involved.

The benefit of this hack is that it helps you identify and fix any potential technical problems before they become big issues during the event. By doing so, you can avoid embarrassing situations, delays, and frustration for both you and your participants.

Here are some additional tips to help you with your tech check:

Make a checklist of all the necessary equipment, software, and tools you need for your event, and test them thoroughly.

Check your internet connection speed and stability. You can use online tools such as Speedtest.net to check your bandwidth.

If you are using new software or tools, take some time to learn how to use them before the event. Have a backup plan in case something goes wrong. For example, have a backup internet connection or a backup laptop ready.

Make sure you have all the relevant contact information of your support team, such as IT support, customer service, or technical support.

By following these tips and doing a thorough tech check, you can ensure a seamless and successful remote workshop.

Hack #88: Check the technology.

#89 - Avoid Pre-Reading Before A Workshop

Why You Shouldn't Waste Your Time (or Your Participants') with Unnecessary Preparations.

Let us face it: we have all been there. You sign up for a virtual workshop, only to be bombarded with pages upon pages of pre-reading material that you will never get around to reading. And if you do manage to squeeze it in, chances are you will forget half of what you read by the time the actual session rolls around. So, what is the point?

The truth is, in the fast-paced corporate world, most people simply do not have the time (or the inclination) to pore over mountains of pre-reading material. And even if some do, there is always the risk that they'll get distracted or forget what they've read before the session even starts.

Very often, it is only about 10-20% who complete the task or preparation. What will you do later in the workshop? If you run the session relying on the prework, you will lose those who have not done it. If you do a quick recap of what the prep was about, you will frustrate those who invested the time prepping.

That is why you should ditch the pre-reading altogether. Instead, focus on creating engaging, interactive sessions that do not rely on pre-work to be effective. Sure, you can provide some basic background information or a quick summary of what you will be covering, but don't expect your participants to be experts on the topic before they even show up.

By eliminating the need for pre-reading, you will not only save yourself time and effort, but you will also make your sessions more accessible and inclusive for everyone. No one will feel left out or frustrated because they did not have time to complete the pre-work, and everyone will be on the same page (literally) when the session begins.

Hack #89: Do not rely on pre-reading for your workshops.

#90 - Avoid Homework After A Workshop

No Additional Tasks, Please!

We are all busy bees, and the last thing we want to do after a long day of work is more work. Asking participants to complete homework assignments after or between sessions may seem like a clever idea in theory, but in reality, most people will not do it. And can you blame them? They have families to take care of, hobbies to pursue, and Netflix shows to binge-watch. So, if you want to make your remote workshop a success, do not rely on homework activities.

Instead, focus on making your sessions engaging and interactive. Use breakout rooms, polls, and other online tools to keep your participants on their toes. And if you want to provide additional resources for those who want to learn more, offer some "further reading" content. This way, you are giving people the option to dig deeper if they choose to, without overwhelming them with homework assignments.

By ditching the traditional homework model, you will make your remote workshop more accessible and enjoyable for everyone involved. Plus, you will be able to ensure that all participants are on the same page, rather than leaving some behind because they did not have time to do their homework.

Example: Let us say you're running a virtual leadership development program for a group of managers. Instead of assigning homework, you could use a case study exercise during the session.

Break participants into small groups and give them a real-life scenario to analyze and solve together. This not only keeps the session engaging but also helps participants apply what they have learned in a practical way.

And if you want to offer further reading, provide some articles or TED talks on leadership that participants can access in their own time.

Hack #90: Skip the homework after a workshop or in between sessions.

#91 - Breakouts Secret 8: Quick Pulse Check

Breakout Snooping: The Secret to Successful Group Exercises.

When you are running a remote workshop with breakouts, do not just set the breakout rooms and forget about them. Instead, sneak into each room briefly after opening them to make sure everything is running smoothly.

Why do this? Well, as a facilitator, you want to make sure that your participants are able to work together effectively in their breakout rooms. Maybe someone's having technical difficulties, or they're not sure what they're supposed to be doing, or they're just not gelling as a group. By checking in on each room, you can quickly spot any issues and intervene before they become big problems.

Of course, you do not want to be intrusive or disrupt the flow of the session, so keep your visits brief and unobtrusive. Just pop in, say hello, ask if anyone needs help, and then leave. You'll be amazed at how much smoother your remote workshops will run when you use this simple but effective hack.

For example, let's say you're running a virtual brainstorming session with several breakout rooms, and you notice that one of the rooms is completely silent. You pop in and realize that the participants are all stuck on one idea and aren't sure how to move forward. By quickly intervening and providing some guidance, you are able to get them back on track and ensure that they're able to contribute meaningfully to the session.

So don't be afraid to be a little bit sneaky - it could make all the difference to the success of your remote workshops!

Hack #91: Do a quick check if all is fine after sending people to breakouts.

#92 - Shorten Your Teaching Slots

Stop Lecturing: Keep Your Audience Awake with Bite-Sized Engagement.

Nobody likes being talked to for extended periods of time, especially in virtual workshops. So why subject your audience to a dull, dreary lecture when you can keep them alert and engaged with bite-sized bursts of interaction?

By limiting your "teach" slots to the bare minimum and breaking up longer segments with regular engagement, you'll be able to maintain the attention of your audience throughout your entire session. This could be accomplished through brief questions, thought-provoking statements, video clips, changing media formats, polls, chat, and more.

Why is this important? Well, research has shown that the average attention span for virtual learning is in the range of 10 minutes. So, if you want to keep your participants on their toes, it is important to break up your content into bite-sized chunks.

For example, let's say you're leading a virtual workshop on effective communication in the workplace. Instead of droning on for 30-45 minutes about the importance of active listening, you could break up the lesson into a series of a few 5–10-minute mini-lectures. During each segment, you could ask the audience a question, show a video clip of effective communication in action, or prompt them to discuss their own experiences in the chat.

With this hack, you'll keep your virtual participants engaged and energized throughout the entire session, ensuring they walk away with lasting knowledge and a sense of satisfaction.

Hack #92: Limit your teaching slots to the unavoidable minimum.

#93 - Breakouts Secret 9: Camera Off When Joining

The Silent Observer: How to Enter a Virtual Room Like a Ninja.

Imagine you are in the middle of an intense brainstorming session with your team, and suddenly someone enters the room and says "hello." It is the facilitator, and now everyone's attention is diverted, and the flow is interrupted. This is a common scenario in virtual meetings, but there is a hack to avoid it: the silent observer.

Before the meeting starts, let your team know that you may join their sessions without announcing yourself. Then, when you do enter the virtual room, turn off your camera and simply observe. This way, the participants will not get distracted by your arrival, and you can get a sense of how the conversation is going without disrupting the flow.

By being a silent observer, you can notice the dynamics of the team, notice any issues that need addressing, and provide more targeted feedback. Plus, it shows your team that you trust them to carry on without you and can even create a sense of autonomy.

For example, let us say you're facilitating a remote team-building activity. You want to see how well the participants are working together without your guidance. By being a silent observer, you can observe their interactions and adjust your facilitation accordingly. You may notice that some participants are hesitant to speak up or that there is a power imbalance that needs addressing.

In conclusion, the silent observer hack allows you to be a fly on the wall without disrupting the meeting's natural flow. It is a small adjustment that can make a big difference in the quality of your remote facilitation.

Hack #93: Camera off when sneaking into a breakout room.

#94 - Disable All Notification Pop-Ups

Clear Mind, Clean Desk: Avoid Embarrassing Moments During Your Workshop.

To run a successful remote session, it is crucial to eliminate all potential distractions. One of the biggest culprits? Those annoying notification pop-ups that can not only derail your focus, but also potentially embarrass you in front of your participants. Imagine leading a workshop on effective communication skills, only to have a personal email notification pop up with a subject line that says, "Getting dumped...again?" Yikes!

Or imagine you are leading a remote workshop on project management, and suddenly a notification (from your manager) pops up on your screen that says, "Let's talk about your performance tonight." Not only could this distract you from the task at hand, but it could also be embarrassing if your participants catch a glimpse of the notification. And mumbling something like "This is not what it looks like" does not fix the situation and can make things even worse.

To avoid such cringe-worthy moments, it is important to switch off all notification pop-ups before starting your remote workshop. Additionally, make sure to close any windows or tabs with private content that you do not want your participants to see. By doing so, you create a clean and distraction-free workspace that allows you to focus solely on facilitating a successful workshop.

***

Hack #94: Clean up your desk, close unnecessary windows and turn off all notification pop-ups.

***

#95 - Build Rapport Using Eye Contact

The Eye Contact Trick: How to Connect with Your Virtual Audience.

In virtual meetings and workshops, creating a genuine connection with your audience can be challenging, especially when it comes to making eye contact. But fear not, there is a simple hack to make your eye contact seem more natural and personal. Instead of looking at your participants' video images on your screen, look at the camera lens. This way, your gaze will appear to be making eye contact with your audience, even though you are not looking at their faces.

The benefit of this hack is that it helps create a more intimate and engaging connection with your virtual audience. When you are looking directly at them, participants are more likely to feel seen, heard, and valued. This can lead to increased engagement, participation, and retention of information.

Let us say you're leading a virtual training session on a new software tool. You want to make sure your participants feel comfortable asking questions and sharing their thoughts. By using the eye contact trick, you will be able to create a more personal and inviting atmosphere. As you explain the software, you can look directly at the camera lens, making it seem like you're speaking directly to each participant.

When a participant asks a question, you can continue to make eye contact with the lens as you answer, giving the impression of a one-on-one conversation. An additional hack to help you remember the camera lens trick, place a smiley next to the camera. And the smiling icon does another trick as well: it also reminds you to smile more often - which makes you come across much more likable.

Hack #95: Look into the camera lens if you want to look into the eyes of your participants.

#96 - Use A Living Screenplay

Script Your Way to Success with a Living Agenda.

As a facilitator, you know that time management is key to running a successful remote workshop. But how do you ensure that you stay on track and keep the session flowing smoothly? The answer is simple: use a living script!

Just like a screenplay for a movie, a script for your workshop can help you map out the flow of activities and keep everyone on track. To make sure your script is effective, aim for a granularity of 5 minutes per step, and block out your activities in 10, 15, or 20-minute increments. This will help you keep the pace of the session moving and avoid any awkward pauses or lulls in the conversation. But most importantly: make it a living document! As workshops never run exactly as planned, you need to constantly adjust your script and change the timing, delete, or add steps.

One of the main benefits of using a living script is that it helps you stay in control of the session. You will always know what's coming next, which means you can easily guide the discussion and steer it back on course if it starts to veer off track. Plus, with a script at your fingertips, you will not need to rely on your memory or worry about forgetting an important point.

There are several ways to create a script that works for you. Some facilitators prefer to print out a hard copy and keep it on their desk, while others prefer to use an online tool like SessionLab. Whatever method you choose, make sure your script is easy to read, easy to adjust on the fly and always within reach.

Hack #96: Use a living script to keep control of the timing.

#97 - Follow-Up

Do not Let Your Workshop Fizzle Out: Ensure Proper Follow-Up with These Simple Steps.

So, you have just hosted an amazing virtual workshop - high-fives all around! But wait, what happens next? Without proper follow-up, all that effort you put into facilitating the workshop can fizzle out, leaving your participants feeling disconnected and unmotivated.

That is where this hack comes in. By assigning owners to specific topics and scheduling follow-up checkpoints, you will ensure that the momentum you built during the workshop keeps going strong. Assigning owners means that each topic or action item has someone responsible for making sure it gets done. And scheduling follow-up checkpoints ensures that everyone stays on track and accountable.

For example, let's say you've just facilitated a workshop on customer service. You can assign the topic of "responding to customer complaints" to one participant and the topic of "creating a customer feedback survey" to another. Then, schedule a checkpoint a month from now to follow up on their progress and discuss any challenges they've encountered.

With this hack, you'll not only keep your participants engaged and motivated, but you'll also ensure that your workshop has a lasting impact on their work. Don't let all your hard work go to waste - use this hack to ensure proper follow-up and keep the momentum going strong.

Hack #97: Ensure proper follow-up activities.

#98 - Breakouts Secret 10: The Right Mix

Mix it Up or Stick Together? Deciding on Breakout Groups.

When running sub-sequential breakout sessions in a virtual event, you need to decide whether to stick with the same teams or switch them up. The answer? It depends on your goals for the event.

If your aim is to provide consistency and avoid the hassle of participants having to find their teammates in each new breakout, it is best to keep the teams the same. Ensure that the groups are large enough to account for potential dropouts. On the other hand, if your focus is on fostering networking and encouraging participants to meet new colleagues, it is better to switch up the teams in each new breakout.

By carefully considering whether to stick or switch, you can tailor your breakout sessions to better achieve your desired outcomes. Consistency can provide a sense of familiarity and ease for participants, while switching up teams can encourage new connections and collaboration.

Hack #98: Change the participants in subsequent Breakout Groups if you want to maximize creating new connections. And keep them the same if you need consistency and minimal distraction.

#99 - Connecting People (Revisited)

Connection after Content.

You know what they say, "It's not what you know, it's who you know." So why not leverage your remote workshop and create a network of connected individuals? After all, your participants are not just there to absorb information, they are there to meet like-minded people, expand their networks, and grow their careers.

That is where "Connection after Content" comes in. Instead of rushing to wrap up your workshop after delivering the content, share some thoughts about how to also make this a networking session. Share the contact details of all participants on a virtual whiteboard or in a shared document and encourage them to reach out to one another after the workshop.

The benefits are twofold: first, it helps build a sense of community among participants, which is particularly important when working remotely. Second, it creates an opportunity for participants to connect with professionals from other organizations, which can lead to valuable collaborations, partnerships, or job opportunities.

Hack #99: Build connections that last.

#100 - Avoid Lengthy Feedback Rounds

Bye-bye Boring Feedback: The One-Sentence Solution.

Let us face it, nobody wants to sit through a long and tedious feedback round at the end of a remote workshop. It is repetitive, time-consuming, and frankly, a little bit boring.

So why not mix it up and ask your participants to type just one sentence into the chat? It could be their key takeaway, what they liked or disliked the most, or even just a simple emoji. Or have them type a rating into the chat, asking: "How valuable has this been to you?" With a rating from 1-10. This is quick, it is easy, and it provides valuable insights into how your participants are feeling.

But do not stop there! Use a formal survey like with SurveyMonkey or similar tools (or just via old-school e-mail) as a follow-up step to collect more detailed feedback. This will give you even more insight into what worked and what did not, and you can use these statements to market your future workshops.

By streamlining the feedback process, you will save time and energy while still getting the feedback you need to improve your remote workshops. So, say goodbye to the boring feedback round and hello to the one-sentence solution!

Hack #100: Avoid lengthy feedback rounds at the end. And use one-sentence feedback in the chat and formal surveys for real insight.

#101 - Simply Be You

Authenticity is Key: Don't Fake it in Your Virtual Workshops.

Finally, here is our last of the 101 facilitation hacks. And perhaps the most important one.

We have all seen those cringe-worthy virtual workshops where the facilitator tries too hard to be someone they are not. Do not be that person. Authenticity is key when it comes to virtual facilitation. Your participants want to connect with YOU, not some imitation of another facilitator they have seen online.

By being authentic, you will build trust with your participants and create a safe space for them to engage in meaningful discussions. You will also be able to bring your unique strengths and talents to the table, which will set you apart from the crowd.

For example, let us say you are facilitating a virtual brainstorming session. Instead of trying to imitate a well-known TED speaker, tap into your own creativity and brainstorming techniques. Share your own experiences and stories to inspire your participants and encourage them to think outside the box.

So, do not fall into the trap of trying to be someone you're not. Embrace your own style, find your strengths, and develop your brand in a way that is authentic to YOU. Your virtual workshops will be more engaging, effective, and memorable as a result.

Hack #101: Be authentic. Be you.

Take Your Skills to the Next Level: Bonus Content

Congratulations on reaching the end of 101 Remote Collaboration Hacks! By now, you've learned a lot about how to work effectively with remote teams, communicate clearly, and use technology to your advantage. But there's more to remote collaboration than just the basics.

In this chapter, we'll take a deeper dive into the world of remote collaboration and explore some additional content that can help you take your skills to the next level. We've included a range of resources that can help you improve your remote collaboration skills, including our favorite tools, icebreakers, questions to ask, and pre-built agendas.

Whether you're a remote work veteran or new to the game, this bonus content can provide you with valuable resources and insights to help you succeed. So, let's dive in and discover how you can enhance your remote collaboration skills and achieve even greater success with your virtual teams.

Video, Audio, Room Setup Recommendations

Video and Lighting

Video

Use a high-quality webcam that can capture video in at least 1080p resolution. This will provide clear and crisp video for participants. Position the camera at eye level to create a more natural and engaging experience for participants. To optimize the camera perspective, it is recommended to adjust the frame so that the top of the head is almost touching the upper edge of the screen, while still keeping the shoulders visible. This will allow for the hands to be visible and utilized during the session.

Make sure the camera is steady and won't wobble during the session. Consider using a tripod or stabilizer to ensure stability. Also ensure the camera is in focus and adjust the settings to improve clarity and quality.

Using two cameras can provide more flexibility and a better viewing experience for participants. One camera can be used for the speaker or presenter, while the other can be used to display other visuals, such as slides or a whiteboard. This can enhance engagement and make the presentation more dynamic.

However, to use two cameras, you will need software that can switch between the two feeds seamlessly. This can be done with many video conferencing platforms, or you can use dedicated video switching software such as OBS or ManyCam.

Lighting

Whenever possible, try to use natural lighting by positioning yourself in front of a window or in a well-lit room. This will provide clear and even lighting that is flattering and easy on the eyes. It's extremely important to avoid sitting with a window or light source behind you, as this can create a shadowed or backlit effect.

If natural lighting isn't available, don't use the light from the ceiling or any other harsh or direct light source that can create unflattering shadows. To create diffuse light, photographers often use a softbox, which is typically a large, rectangular box-shaped structure that is covered with a diffuse, translucent material such as nylon or polyester. It is usually mounted on a light stand and contains one or more light bulbs or flash units inside, which are aimed at the material to produce a soft and even light.

Alternatively, LED lights are energy-efficient and often come with adjustable brightness and color temperature. Warm white light color is beneficial because it creates a comfortable and inviting atmosphere, which can help to put people at ease and enhance the overall quality of the virtual session. Consider the amount of space you have available for the lighting setup as well, since soft box lights require more space and can be more difficult to set up than LED lights.

LED lights can be a very good low-budget solution. Ring lights are available for just a few bucks with good enough quality. However, if you wear glasses, we recommend using flat rectangular devices, as ring lights can create circles of light on glasses, which can be distracting.

To achieve optimal lighting for your video, we suggest using LED lights or softboxes, even if you have natural daylight in your room. Softboxes or LED lights can help to reduce harsh shadows caused by direct sunlight on your face, resulting in a more visually pleasing appearance.

Also, take the color of the room's walls into consideration since this can impact the lighting as well. White walls can reflect light, while dark walls can absorb it, resulting in a darker and less flattering image.

Ensure that the lighting is consistent throughout the session to avoid any distractions.

When dressing for the session, wear professional attire and avoid bright or distracting colors that can be overwhelming on camera. Test your camera and lighting before the session to make sure everything is working correctly and make any necessary adjustments to achieve the best possible outcome.

Audio

Audio is just as important as video in virtual sessions. To ensure clear and high-quality sound, there are a few things to keep in mind.

Firstly, the built-in microphone on your computer or laptop is not recommended as it tends to pick up background noise and may not provide the best sound quality. Instead, we recommend using an external microphone. There are several options to choose from, including condenser, dynamic, boom, lavalier, or typical headsets.

A condenser microphone is a high-quality option that captures sound with great detail and sensitivity, making it ideal for recording music or voice-overs. However, it is very sensitive to background noise, so it should only be used in a quiet environment.

Dynamic microphones are more durable and resistant to handling noise than condenser mics. They are also better suited for environments with a lot of background noise, but they may not pick up as much detail as condenser mics. Dynamic microphones are often used in podcasts and produce decent sound quality even at lower price tags. Keep in mind that they can be bulky, expensive, and may need to be positioned close to your mouth, which could be distracting in a video and impede your movements.

A boom microphone is a directional mic that is mounted on a long arm, allowing you to position it in a direct line to your mouth outside of the video frame. However, they are very sensitive to your position and can affect sound quality if you move around.

A lavalier microphone, also known as a lapel mic, is a small, discreet microphone that can be clipped onto clothing. It is a great compromise between sound quality, background noise, and having no distracting device in front of you. They are also sensitive enough to allow to play background music coming from an external speaker in your room. In 90% of cases, this thing is perfect. It's small, super cheap, looks professional (!) and still has very good sound quality, even at price tags below 10 bucks.

Headsets are a popular option for virtual sessions due to their ability to provide high-quality sound and minimize background noise. One significant advantage of headsets is their excellent sound absorption, which can reduce distractions from external noise sources such as children, dogs, or construction work. Also, other people around you are not disturbed much.

However, they can be distracting visually and may not be comfortable for extended sessions. Additionally, their association with business meetings can limit the ability to create a unique and engaging atmosphere for workshops or training sessions. Wearing headphones can help you monitor your audio and prevent echo or feedback. However, it can also be uncomfortable for long periods of time and may not be necessary if you have good quality external speakers; most virtual conferencing tools have very good built-in echo cancellations anyway, which makes to use of headphones obsolete for this purpose. We recommend using external speakers for your device setup, as laptop speakers tend to be of lower quality and can cause ear fatigue with prolonged use.

When setting up your audio, it's important to consider the room you're in. Room reverb can affect the quality of your sound, so it's recommended to choose a quiet, well-insulated room. If you're in a room with hard surfaces, such as tile or hardwood floors, consider using a carpet or rug to absorb sound.

Room Setup

The room setup for virtual sessions is also an important consideration, not only for sound reasons. The background behind you should be clean and free of clutter or distracting elements. A plain wall or a bookshelf with neatly arranged books can make for a good background. Avoid busy or brightly colored backgrounds that can be distracting or unprofessional.

To clean up your background, an often-discussed option is to use a greenscreen. We only recommend this option if you are a bit of a nerd who loves to fiddle around with additional software like OBS and tons of parameters. Greenscreens require perfect lighting and some experience with chroma key handling. There are a few virtual conferencing tools which work properly with greenscreens, but most don't.

Much simpler alternatives are roll-up banners or transportable, thin partition walls behind you. This is a simple hack that helps create a more professional and polished appearance. One of the authors simply screwed an opaque gray window shade to the ceiling, which he can pull down when needed in front of his wall of books behind him.

In terms of the desk in front of you, make sure it is clean and organized. Avoid having too many items on the desk, especially if they are not relevant to the session. A lamp, a notebook, and a pen are sufficient items to have on the desk.

Using two monitors during virtual sessions can increase productivity and make it easier to access all necessary documents or applications. However, it's important to consider the layout of the monitors. Position them at eye level, and make sure that there is no glare or reflection from external light sources.

If you have a height-adjustable table, you can use this to support your body language during the sessions. It makes a difference whether you sit or stand in front of the camera (what means in front of your participants who usually all sit during the session).

Top 10 Remote Icebreakers

Using icebreakers is an effective way to set the tone for a productive and engaging meeting. By doing so, you create a relaxed atmosphere where people feel comfortable sharing their thoughts and ideas. This helps to build rapport among the participants and fosters a sense of connection that can be difficult to achieve in a virtual setting.

Here are ten great icebreakers and warmup exercises to get your remote meetings off to a flying start.

Two Truths and a Lie

Each participant shares two true statements and one false statement about themselves, and the group must guess which one is the lie. This icebreaker encourages participants to share a bit about themselves while also challenging their peers to guess which statement is false. It can help build trust and create a more relaxed atmosphere.

Personal Scavenger Hunt

Participants must find items around their house that match a certain description (e.g., something blue, something round) and share them with the group. This activity encourages participants to find commonalities with their peers. It can also create a more interactive and engaging environment.

Virtual Office Tour

Participants give a virtual tour of their workspace and share fun facts about themselves. This icebreaker allows participants to share a bit about their personal life and create a more intimate environment. It can also help create a sense of familiarity and comfort among the group.

It is important to note that this icebreaker may be intrusive for those who do not have a separate office and instead use their living room, for example. Therefore, it is essential to adapt or modify the activity to ensure all participants feel comfortable and included. Additionally, this icebreaker may be more applicable for teams that have already established a level of trust.

Would You Rather

Ask participants to choose between two options and explain their reasoning, like "if you had a time machine, would you rather jump back to the past or into the future?" This activity encourages participants to share their opinions and thought processes. It can help create a more interactive and engaging environment while also revealing commonalities and differences among participants.

One-Word Check-In

Each participant shares one word, an emoji or an animated gif that describes how they are feeling that day. This icebreaker allows participants to share their current mood or state of mind in a quick and easy way. It can help create a more positive and supportive environment.

Photo Sharing

Participants share a photo that represents something they are looking forward to in the near future. This activity encourages participants to share a bit about their personal life and create a more intimate environment. It can also reveal shared interests and goals among the group.

Creative Writing

Participants are given a prompt and a set amount of time to draft a short story or poem, and then share with the group. This icebreaker encourages participants to be creative and think outside the box. It can help create a more engaging and interactive environment while also revealing individual strengths and interests.

Desert Island

Participants are stranded on a desert island and have to choose three items to bring with them. This activity encourages participants to think strategically and creatively. It can also reveal shared interests and priorities among the group.

This or That

Participants choose between two options (e.g., cats or dogs) and explain why they made their choice. This icebreaker encourages participants to share their opinions and thought processes. It can help create a more interactive and engaging environment while also revealing commonalities and differences among participants.

Who Am I?

Participants write down a famous person or fictional character on a piece of paper and then hold it up to their camera. The group has to guess who they are. This activity encourages participants to be creative and think outside the box. It can also create a more interactive and engaging environment while also revealing individual interests and personalities.

By using these icebreakers, you can create a fun and engaging atmosphere that encourages participation and sets the stage for a productive meeting.

Our 3 Favorite Icebreakers

Out of these ten icebreakers, the three that we personally use the most often are **One-Word Check-In, Would You Rather** and **Photo Sharing**.

We often use **One-Word Check-In** in the first few minutes of the session by asking the question, "How do you feel this morning?" and instructing participants to answer in the chat.

We frequently use **Would You Rather** with participants who have their camera turned on. We ask, "Would you rather drink tea forever or coffee? Show one finger if you choose tea or two fingers if you choose coffee."

Photo Sharing is something we use regularly when we want to stimulate storytelling. This icebreaker has two other positive side effects: if we ask people so use real photos, they have to turn the camera on to share them with the audience. On virtual whiteboards we ask the participants to search for images on the web and to put them on the board, for example next to a picture of themselves. This helps to get them acquainted with the virtual whiteboard.

Top 10 Connection Before Content Questions

In remote facilitation, it is easy to dive right into the meat of your session without taking the time to build connections with your participants. But if you want to create a truly engaging and impactful virtual workshop, it is important to prioritize building rapport first.

Here are 10 great questions to build connections with your participants. You can use chat as well as microphones, depending on the size of the group.

What could you talk about for hours?

By asking this question, you can learn about participants' interests and passions. It can also help create a more relaxed atmosphere and allow participants to feel more comfortable opening up.

What brings you to this workshop today?

This question allows participants to share their motivation for attending the workshop. Understanding their reasons can help you tailor the content to better meet their needs and goals.

What is one thing you are hoping to gain from this session?

Asking about participants' expectations for the session can help them set intentions and stay engaged throughout the workshop. It can also allow you to clarify any misunderstandings or expectations upfront.

What is one thing you are proud of accomplishing recently?

Celebrating small victories can be an important motivator for participants. Sharing their accomplishments can also help build confidence and establish a more positive and supportive environment.

What is one thing you are struggling with right now?

This question allows participants to share any difficulties they may be experiencing. It can also help you tailor the content to better address their needs and provide support where necessary.

What is one thing you are looking forward to in the coming weeks/months?

By discussing upcoming events or plans, you can help create a more positive and engaging atmosphere. It can also reveal shared interests and commonalities between participants.

What is the story of your name?

Asking about the story of someone's name is a great question that can build a sense of connection and community by fostering personal connection and highlighting cultural diversity.

What is one thing you are currently reading/watching/listening to?

Asking about current media consumption can create a more relaxed and casual environment. It can also lead to interesting discussions and recommendations among participants.

What is a goal you have for yourself in the next year?

This question encourages participants to think about their long-term aspirations and can help you tailor the content to address their goals. It can also provide insight into their priorities and interests.

What is one thing you are grateful for today?

By focusing on gratitude, you can create a more positive and supportive atmosphere. Expressing gratitude has been shown to improve overall well-being and happiness, which can improve engagement and participation.

All these questions help build rapport with your participants which creates a sense of trust and connection. This can lead to more meaningful discussions and a more engaged audience. By taking the time to get to know your participants and allowing them to get to know each other, you'll create a more supportive and collaborative virtual environment.

Our 3 Favorite Questions

Out of these ten questions, the three that we personally use the most often are:

What could you talk about for hours? This is by far our favorite question to start a session with as people love discussing their passions without feeling directly asked about them.

What is one thing you are currently reading, watching, or listening to? People enjoy sharing their favorite shows, books, or music.

What is the story of your name? This is another positive question that we often use, allowing participants to share a deep, meaningful or an insignificant story about their first, middle, or last name.

Our Favorite Tools

In today's remote work environment, virtual icebreakers and warm-up exercises are essential to build connections, create engagement, and foster collaboration among team members. Fortunately, there are many digital tools available that can help make these activities more engaging, fun, and interactive. In this chapter, we will explore some of our favorite tools that can be used for icebreakers, interaction, fun, and collaboration.

Mentimeter, Slido, And Alike

Mentimeter, Slido and AhaSlides are popular digital tools for engaging remote teams during meetings, conferences, and workshops. These tools offer a range of interactive features, including live polls, quizzes, word clouds, and Q&A sessions. Participants can respond to these activities in real-time using their mobile devices or computers, making it easier to break the ice and initiate discussions. These three tools are user-friendly, customizable, and offer real-time data analysis, making them great for remote facilitation.

Mentimeter: https://www.mentimeter.com/
Slido: https://www.sli.do/
AhaSlides: https://ahaslides.com

Picker Wheel

Picker Wheel is a free online tool that can be used for random selection and decision-making. The tool allows users to create a wheel with customized options and spin it to generate a random selection.

This tool can be used to select participants for icebreakers, group activities, or brainstorming sessions, making it an effective way to involve everyone in the discussion and break the ice. The Picker Wheel is one of our favorite tools.

Picker Wheel: https://pickerwheel.com/

Icebreaker.range.co

Icebreaker.range.co is a virtual platform that offers a range of icebreaker activities for remote teams. The platform includes fun and interactive games such as Trivia, Bingo, and Word Association. These games can be customized based on team size, interests, and goals, making it an effective way to break the ice and create engagement.

Icebreaker Range: https://icebreaker.range.co/

Warmupz.com

Warmupz.com is a web-based platform that offers a range of icebreaker games and activities. The platform includes virtual games such as Two Truths and a Lie, Never Have I Ever, and Pictionary. These games can be used to create a fun and interactive atmosphere, making it easier for team members to connect and collaborate remotely.

Warmupz: https://warmupz.com/

Find even more links, tools, playlists, and icebreakers here:

www.innovation-hackers.de/links

How to Deal with "Stupid" Questions?

Let us be real, we have all been in a meeting or workshop where someone asks a question that seems so basic or irrelevant, we can't help but roll our eyes or let out a sigh. But these so-called "stupid" questions can be the key to unlocking new insights and ideas. Here are ten best practices to help you deal with the "stupid" questions:

Use The Parking Lot

This allows you to acknowledge the question without derailing the current topic, and it also ensures that the question is not forgotten. You can then address these questions at an appropriate time later in the session, or even in a follow-up email or communication.

Reframe The Question

Instead of dismissing a question outright, try reframing it in a way that makes it more relevant to the topic at hand.

Use The Question To Clarify

Sometimes what may seem like a "stupid" question is simply a request for clarification. Take the time to provide a clear and concise answer.

Explore The Underlying Assumptions

A question that seems silly on the surface may be challenging assumptions that everyone else is taking for granted. Take the opportunity to explore these assumptions and see where this question leads.

Encourage Curiosity

Instead of shutting down "stupid" questions, use them to spark curiosity and encourage others to think outside the box.

Use Humor

Sometimes a little humor can go a long way in diffusing tension and encouraging people to open up.

Acknowledge The Question

Even if you do not have an immediate answer to a "stupid" question, take the time to acknowledge it and let the person know that you will come back to it later.

Pass It To The Participants

Often, the best answers come not from the facilitator, but from the group. Encourage participants to share their own experiences and insights.

Foster A Growth Mindset

Remind participants that everyone is here to learn and grow, and that asking questions is an important part of that process.

Remember The Big Picture

When faced with a "stupid" question, it can be easy to get bogged down in the details. Keep your eye on the big picture and remember that every question, no matter how silly it may seem, is an opportunity to learn and grow.

How to Deal with Difficult People?

Dealing with difficult people can be challenging, especially in a virtual workshop setting where communication is limited to online tools. However, with the right mindset and approach, facilitators can turn even the most challenging participants into productive contributors. Here are our ten best practices for handling difficult people in virtual workshops:

Coolness Wins

Stay calm and do not take things personally. Difficult people often act out of frustration, so try to be patient and understanding.

Set Ground Rules

Set ground rules at the beginning of the workshop. This will establish expectations and help prevent difficult behavior from the outset.

Use Positive Language

Use positive language and reinforce positive behavior. This will encourage difficult people to follow suit and improve their behavior.

Use Active Listening

Listen actively and show empathy. Difficult people often just want to be heard, so take the time to listen and understand their point of view.

Get Help From The Team

Encourage participation from all attendees. This will help to prevent difficult people from dominating the conversation.

Adapt Your Communication Style

Be flexible and adapt to different communication styles. Different people have different communication preferences, so try to be accommodating and flexible.

Use Humor

Use humor to diffuse tension. A well-timed joke or quip can often lighten the mood and help to defuse a tricky situation.

Use The Break

Provide regular breaks and opportunities for attendees to recharge. This will help to prevent fatigue and frustration from setting in.

Have A Personal Conversation

Use private chat to communicate with difficult people one-on-one. This can be a useful way to address specific concerns without disrupting the flow of the workshop.

Follow Up

Follow up after the workshop to address any outstanding issues or concerns. This will demonstrate that you care about the participants and are committed to their success.

By mastering the art of handling difficult people in virtual workshops, facilitators can improve engagement, productivity, and overall success of the workshop. By applying these best practices, facilitators can prevent difficult people from derailing the workshop and encourage all participants to contribute to the fullest extent possible.

Biggest Fails - Things Will Go Wrong

Anything that can go wrong, probably will. But that does not mean you should just cross your fingers and hope for the best. You should be prepared for the worst.

You need to expect the unexpected. Here are some nice little funny stories that were shared with us where facilitators had unexpected things happening to them but handled them well.

The Zoom Filter Faux Pas

During a virtual session, the facilitator accidentally left a funny filter on his video camera, making him look like talking broccoli. The attendees found it hilarious and started asking questions about the filter. The facilitator was a bit embarrassed in the first place but relaxed quickly and turned the situation into a fun icebreaker activity, where attendees had to guess which filter the facilitator was using next.

The Child Interrupts

During a virtual session, a facilitator's child burst into the room and started asking for help with their homework. The facilitator was caught off guard, but quickly muted himself and attended to his child's needs. To make light of the situation, he turned it into an icebreaker activity, where attendees had to share their funniest stories of being interrupted during a virtual meeting. Such a situation - if handled properly - can make you appear much more human and can build strong personal bridges for all other people who have similar challenges working from home.

The Doorbell Dilemma

In this story a facilitator was leading a global virtual training session, her doorbell rang repeatedly. The facilitator apologized and excused her to answer the door. She was wearing one of these jack-mics with a wireless connector as she liked to move around in the room while teaching. Accidentally she forgot to mute herself and broadcasted her conversation with the delivery driver, who was lost and asking for directions. When the facilitator realized the mishap, she turned the situation into an impromptu activity, where attendees had to use their problem-solving skills to help a lost traveler to find their way in a foreign country, unable to speak the local language. Later she thought: good luck that she had to go to the door and not to the bathroom.

The Cat Came To Visit

During a virtual session, the cat of a moderator who was running a team building workshop jumped up onto his keyboard and started typing gibberish in the chat box. The moderator quickly apologized to the attendees and removed the cat from the keyboard, but the attendees found it amusing and began asking questions about the cat. The facilitator went with the flow and started a short icebreaker activity, where attendees shared photos of their own pets.

The Virtual Background Mishap

In this story, a facilitator had experimented with some quirky virtual backgrounds the night before an important training session with some senior executives of his company. Unfortunately, he forgot to switch back to his usual background before he began the course the next morning. As soon as the session began, attendees noticed the odd background and pointed it out to the facilitator. He quickly realized his mistake and felt heavily embarrassed. But a few seconds later he made light of the blunder and turned it into an icebreaker activity. He challenged attendees to search for the wackiest and most creative virtual background and share it with the team. This activity helped lighten the mood and brought some laughter to the session.

You may think "this will not happen to me!" But do not be too sure. You may recall some similar incidents that made it to the public and event went viral:

The Cat Filter: During a virtual court hearing in Texas in 2021, a lawyer accidentally appeared on screen as a cat due to a Zoom filter. The lawyer was initially embarrassed, but quickly explained the situation to the judge and everyone had a good laugh. The video went viral, and the lawyer became known as the "cat lawyer."

The Child Interrupted: In 2017, a political science professor in South Korea was in the middle of a live TV interview when his young daughter burst into the room. The professor tried to continue the interview, but his daughter was persistent and demanded his attention. The video became a viral sensation, and the professor became known as "BBC Dad."

The Accidental Unmute: In 2020, a local government meeting in California was disrupted when an attendee accidentally unmuted themselves and started cursing during a public comment period. The meeting was being live-streamed, and the incident went viral on social media.

So, again: expect the unexpected. The mindset makes the difference here. If you do not bite your teeth into it, trying to force it back to normal, if you can laugh about yourself, if you go with the flow and see the opportunity that every "crisis" brings, you can turn it into something positive. Something that people will remember.

Warmup Yourself

As a remote facilitator, you are the captain of the ship, and you need to be fully prepared before going live. Just like athletes need to warm up before a big game, you too need to warm up before facilitating a session.

Benefits of Doing a Warmup

Doing a proper warmup has several benefits:

Increased Energy Levels

Warmup exercises will increase your heart rate and blood flow, which in turn increases the energy levels.

Improved Focus

Warmup exercises will help you clear the mind and improve focus, enabling you to deliver a better session.

Enhanced Vocal Abilities

The warmup exercises for the voice box and the mouth will help you to improve the tone, pitch, and clarity of your voice.

Reduced Anxiety

Warmup exercises will help reduce anxiety and nervousness, allowing you to feel more confident and in control.

Our Favorite Warmup Exercises

Here is our favorite list of quick and effective warmup exercises. They help you focus, energize your body, and get you into an "on-stage" mindset.

Breathing Exercises

Deep breathing exercises can help calm the nerves, reduce anxiety, and increase oxygen levels in the body. Here is a nice routine that works well:

Sit in a comfortable position and take a deep breath through your nose for four seconds.

Hold your breath for seven seconds.

Exhale through your mouth for eight seconds.

Repeat this cycle for a few minutes.

Vocal Warmup Exercises

These exercises are essential to ensure that your voice is in optimal condition for facilitating the session.

Humming: Hum a tune or a sound for a few minutes. This helps to warm up your vocal cords.

Tongue Twisters: Recite tongue twisters to warm up your mouth and improve diction. For example, "How much wood would a woodchuck chuck if a woodchuck could chuck wood?"

Lip Trills: This exercise is great for warming up your lips, mouth, and vocal cords. Here is how to do it: Place your fingers on your cheeks and push slightly. Relax your lips and blow air through them, creating a buzzing sound. Continue the buzzing sound as you move up and down your vocal range.

Tongue Slides: This exercise is great for warming up your tongue and improving articulation. Start by making a "D" sound, holding it for a few seconds. Slowly slide your tongue down to the "R" sound, then to the "L" sound. Move back up to the "R" sound, then to the "D" sound. Repeat this exercise a few times.

Vocal Sirens: This exercise is great for warming up your entire vocal range. Start with a low pitch and gradually slide up to a high pitch, like a siren. Hold the high pitch for a few seconds, then gradually slide back down to the low pitch. Repeat this exercise a few times, gradually increasing the speed and range.

Vowel Sounds: This exercise is great for warming up your mouth and improving vowel sounds. Start by making an "Ah" sound, holding it for a few seconds. Move on to an "Eh" sound, holding it for a few seconds. Move on to an "Ee" sound, holding it for a few seconds. Repeat this exercise with other vowel sounds like "Oh" and "Oo."

We do these Vocal Warmup Exercises before every single session.

Physical Warmup Exercises

These exercises help to increase blood flow, energy, and focus.

Jumping Jacks: They are a great way to increase the heart rate, get the blood pumping, and energize the body.

Jog in place for 2-3 minutes: This helps to increase your heart rate and oxygen levels, which in turn increases energy levels and focus.

Squats: Squats are a great way to warm up the lower body, increase blood flow to the legs, and improve mobility.

Arm Circles: Arm circles are a great way to warm up the upper body, increase blood flow to the arms, and improve shoulder mobility.

Mindset Warmup Exercises

These exercises are great for boosting confidence, improving body language, and increasing energy levels.

The Magic Mirror: Stand in front of a mirror and smile at yourself for 30 seconds. Smiling releases endorphins, which are natural mood boosters. Make eye contact with yourself in the mirror for 30 seconds. This helps to build confidence and establish a strong presence.

Power Pose: Stand with your feet shoulder-width apart, arms at your sides, and take a deep breath in. As you exhale, lift your arms out to your sides and up to the sky, stretching as high as you can. Hold this pose for 30 seconds, imagining that you are strong and confident. This power pose helps to reduce stress and increase confidence.

Affirmation: These are positive statements that can help you shift your mindset and increase your confidence. Choose a positive affirmation that resonates with you, such as "I am confident and capable," "I am a skilled facilitator," or "I am ready to deliver a great session."

Visualization Exercises: This is a powerful technique that can help you mentally prepare for the session. Visualize yourself having delivered an exceptional session, getting fantastic feedback from the participants. Recall the feeling that you had when you did a fantastic job.

Checklists - The Unsexy Secret to Success

A checklist is a simple yet effective tool that can aid in staying organized and prepared, while also helping to avoid major mistakes. The following checklist is one we use when preparing for our popular Innovation Masterclass, known as "Delight Mary."

However, it can be applied to a variety of remote facilitation contexts with equal success.

Check Before the Session

Participants

☐ Define the necessary participants:
business experts, tech experts, critics, etc.

☐ Identify any difficult participants.

☐ Clarify the participant invitation process and who is responsible for inviting them.

☐ Decide how participants will be introduced to the workshop.

☐ Uncover customer success criteria and work out the target group.

☐ Define extreme users.

☐ Plan user interviews, if needed. Decide if they will be local or remote and determine the duration.

Technology

☐ Agree on the conference and whiteboard software to be used.

☐ Have a backup tool ready.

☐ Identify who can help in case of technical issues.

☐ Assess the internet connection: Ensure that you have a stable internet connection and assess it before the workshop starts. If the internet connection is unstable, consider using a backup connection or rescheduling the workshop.

Preparation

☐ Prepare everything the evening before to avoid unnecessary stress.

☐ Choose clothes you feel comfortable in front of the camera.

☐ Check your laptop: ensure that you have all the necessary cables, that it is working fine, that the slides are on it, and that the battery is charged.

☐ Have an extra backup online somewhere.

Communication

☐ Decide what needs to be communicated by whom.

☐ Only communicate the rough agenda without the time stamps for the agenda points

☐ Have a preparation call with the key-stakeholder and take notes.

☐ Provide clear instructions in advance: Make sure that participants have clear instructions on how to join the remote workshop, including any software or tools they need to download or install beforehand.

☐ Share materials in advance: Share any necessary materials, such as a workshop agenda or pre-workshop reading, with participants in advance of the workshop. This will help them prepare and ensure that everyone is on the same page.

☐ Consider time zones: If participants are joining from different time zones, be mindful of scheduling the workshop at a time that is convenient for everyone.

Use the innovation tools before the workshop to make it better:

☐ Ask how to delight the participants before, during, and after the workshop.

☐ Conduct a pre-mortem to consider what could go wrong before, during, or after the workshop.

Structure

☐ Plan short 5–10-minute breaks every 90 minutes.

☐ Ask participants about their time constraints and get their commitment to be present throughout.

☐ Structure the workshop: start/end time, breaks, intro, warm-up, and exercises.

First Minutes Before the Session

☐ Have a glass of water or preferred beverage ready.

☐ Ask the first person joining the session to check your video and sound.

☐ Now relax and enjoy the ride.

Check During the Session

Set expectations for participation:

☐ Set clear expectations for participation,

☐ Example: ask participants to have their cameras on during the workshop or require them to actively participate in group activities.

Engage participants:

☐ Constantly use interactive activities and exercises to engage participants and keep them interested throughout the workshop.

Breakouts

☐ Create breakouts of 5-6 people.

☐ Define supporters in every breakout team, including someone to keep track of time and stop discussions, etc.

Introduction Round

☐ Run a short, fun introduction round using one of the questions to connect.

☐ Example: "What is a topic you could talk about without any preparation?"

Fake Confidence

☐ It is normal to feel nervous, but fake confidence and act as if you know what you're doing.

Timing

☐ Do not tell the group the detailed timing of the agenda.

☐ Secretly adjust the time.

Pause vs. Stop

☐ Use the word "Pause" instead of "Stop."

☐ Example: "Let's pause this conversation."

Regular Reflections

☐ Have regular reflections to talk about how much has been achieved.

Communication

☐ Communicate the achievements regularly and praise the participants.

☐ Use thumb-ups, congratulatory messages, and claps to keep up the excitement.

Regular Breaks

☐ Do not forget the regular breaks. The "pee limit" is 90 minutes.

☐ Use short 5–10-minute breaks with music.

Interviews

☐ In interviews, ask about pain points, fears, hopes, and dreams.

Permission

☐ Ask for permission. Example: "Sounds okay?"

Enjoy It

☐ Do not take yourself too seriously and enjoy the workshop.

End

☐ Remind the group about their achievement.

Check After the Session

Stay Online

☐ Stay online after the workshop to answer any questions.

Follow-up

☐ Write down follow-up questions from attendees and answer them promptly.

☐ Offer follow-up support to the key-stakeholder.

☐ Email slides, pictures, and links.

Evaluate the workshop:

☐ After the workshop, evaluate how it went and gather feedback from participants to identify areas for improvement in future workshops.

Sample Agendas

As described before, every problem-solving workshop follows the same structure, no matter how much time we have been given. We use the double diamond presentation of the Design Thinking innovation process that is being used in most innovative companies to solve problems in a structured way. The double diamond presentation clearly separates the problem phase from the solution space.

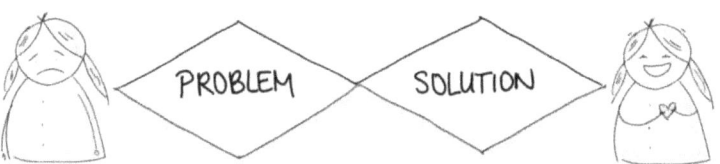

In detail, the double diamond structure consists of four phases:

1. **Discover**: This phase involves understanding the problem space and identifying the pain points of the target group.

2. **Define**: This phase involves defining the problem statement and creating a clear goal for the workshop.

3. **Develop**: This phase involves ideating and prototyping potential solutions.

4. **Deliver**: This phase involves challenging and refining the solutions and creating an action plan for implementation.

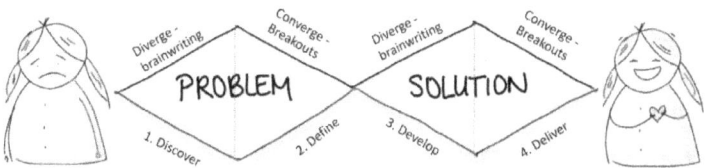

This approach has a couple of advantages:

- It focuses on the pain of the target group (we call her Mary).

- It forces us to create a dream outcome for the target group.

- It separates the problem space from the solution space.

- It separates the divergent from the convergent part in every diamond.

- It makes it clear when to have a break.

- It makes it clear that every workshop needs four elements: **Discover** and **Define** in the problem space and **Develop** and **Deliver** in the solution space.

The double diamond structure with Discover and Define in the problem space and Develop and Deliver in the solution space is ideal for workshops around customer centricity, strategy development, service design, organizational change management, process improvement, team building, user experience (UX) design, product development, and many others.

Regarding the separation of problem and solution space, this basic idea could be used in many situations where there is a need to clarify the problem before jumping into solutions (without the need for a fully-fledged double diamond structure). For example, in personal development, it can be helpful to separate the problem of a situation from the possible solutions before taking action. In project management, it can be useful to separate the problem of a project from the solution by defining the project scope before developing a project plan.

The idea of divergent and convergent phases can be applied in any situation where there is a need to generate ideas (divergent) and then refine and select the best ideas (convergent). For example, in brainstorming sessions, the divergent phase involves generating as many ideas as possible, while the convergent phase involves selecting and refining the best ideas.

In team meetings, the divergent phase may involve open discussion and exploration of ideas, while the convergent phase may involve prioritizing and making decisions based on those ideas.

In summary, the double diamond with divergent and convergent phases is a great blueprint for almost any kind of situation where we are asked to facilitate a workshop - either in its original version or in slightly adjusted formats.

In the next sections we provide sample agendas for such workshops using the double diamond structure.

2-Hour Workshop

This is the minimum amount of time we usually plan for our problem-solving workshops. For teams larger than 8 people we recommend breakout sessions to prioritize results during the convergent steps (Define and Deliver).

Here is a sample agenda for 2-hour workshops:

09:00 - 09:10: Introduction and icebreaker

09:10 - 09:20: Briefing on the double diamond structure and workshop objectives.

09:20 - 09:40: Problem Phase - Discover: Identifying and understanding the problems via interviews and questions.

09:40 - 10:00: Problem Phase - Define: Defining and refining the problem statement and identifying the most important target persona's needs and wants.

10:00 - 10:10: Break

10:10 - 10:40: Solution Phase - Develop: Ideation and brainstorming of workable solutions (e.g., sketching, storyboarding, idea generation)

10:40 - 11:00: Solution Phase - Deliver: Refining the best solution ideas and presenting them back to the group for feedback and refinement. Closing remarks.

4-Hour Workshop

This is the ideal amount of time we usually plan for our problem-solving workshops with a high-level scope. Very often our clients do not allow for more time in the first place. That is why 4 hours are ideal for initial discovery workshops.

Later in the engagement, the clients realize that they need to spend more time on deeper dives or if the problems are bigger and hairier than expected.

Here is a sample agenda for 4-hour workshops:

09:00 - 09:15: Introduction and icebreaker

09:15 - 09:30: Briefing on the double diamond structure and workshop objectives.

09:30 - 10:00: Problem phase - Discover: Identifying and understanding the problem space (e.g., interviews, empathy mapping, problem statement creation)

10:00 - 11:00: Problem phase - Define: Defining and refining the problem statement and identifying the target persona's most important needs and wants.

11:00 - 11:15: Break

11:15 - 12:00: Solution Phase - Develop: Ideation and brainstorming of possible solutions (e.g., sketching, storyboarding, idea generation)

12:00 - 12:45: Solution Phase - Deliver: Refining the best solution ideas and presenting them back to the group for feedback and refinement.

12:45 - 13:00: Closing remarks and next steps.

1-Day Workshop

A full day is a luxury for a virtual workshop, offering enough time to delve deeply into topics and have meaningful discussions without feeling rushed. At the same time, it is still short enough to fit into participants' busy schedules. However, scheduling a full-day workshop typically requires at least 2-3 weeks' notice, and sometimes more.

Here is a sample agenda for 1-day workshops:

09:00 - 09:15: Introduction and icebreaker

09:15 - 09:30: Briefing on the double diamond structure and workshop objectives.

09:30 - 11:30: Problem Phase - Discover: Identifying and understanding the problem space (e.g., empathy mapping, problem statement creation). This should include running interviews with stakeholders to get the outside-in view.

11:30 - 12:30: Problem Phase - Define: Defining and refining the problem statement and identifying the target persona's needs and wants.

12:30 - 13:30: Lunch

13:30 - 15:00: Solution Phase - Develop: Ideation and brainstorming of possible solutions (e.g., sketching, storyboarding, idea generation)

15:00 - 15:15: Break

15:15 - 16:30: Solution Phase - Deliver: Refining the best solution ideas and presenting them back to the group for feedback and refinement.

16:30 - 17:00: Closing remarks and next steps.

1-Day Workshop, Split Over Two Calendar Days

Splitting the one-day virtual workshop into two half-days with an overnight break offers several benefits. Firstly, it is easier to fit into busy schedules. Secondly, it helps to maintain participants' attention, as shorter sessions tend to be more engaging. Additionally, the overnight break provides an opportunity for participants' subconscious minds to continue processing ideas even while they are asleep.

Here is a sample agenda for two half-day workshops:

Day 1:

13:00 - 13:15: Introduction and icebreaker activity

13:15 - 15:15: Problem Phase - Discover: Understanding the problem space and identifying the target persona's pain points and needs. This should include running interviews with stakeholders to get the outside-in view.

15:15 - 15:30: Break

15:30 - 18:00: Problem Phase - Define: Defining and refining the problem statement and identifying the target persona's needs and wants.

Overnight Break

Day 2:

09:00 - 09:15: Recap of Day 1 and agenda for Day 2

09:15 - 10:45: Solution Phase - Develop: Ideation and brainstorming of workable solutions (e.g., sketching, storyboarding, idea generation)

10:45 - 11:00: Break

11:00 - 12:00: Solution Phase – Deliver: Further ideation and refining of ideas, with an emphasis on converging towards the best solutions.

12:00: Closing remarks and next steps.

Any Other Duration

When it comes to longer duration workshops, it is important to remember that there is no one-size-fits-all solution. Each workshop will have its unique goals, challenges, and opportunities. Therefore, a more bespoke approach is required to design and facilitate these workshops.

One key aspect to consider is the scope of the workshop. With more time available, it can be tempting to try to solve all the problems related to a particular issue. However, it is essential to define the scope of the workshop clearly. This means prioritizing the most critical issues, defining what problems you want to solve, and setting achievable goals.

Another important consideration is organization. Longer workshops require more planning and preparation. This includes arranging for comfortable and well-equipped facilities, providing snacks and refreshments, and ensuring that everyone has the necessary materials.

It is also vital to have enough time for stakeholder interviews and research before the workshop. The more time you spend understanding the problem space, the more effective your workshop will be.

This will allow you to identify the pain points of your target group and create a dream outcome that meets their needs.

In summary, longer workshops require a more bespoke approach that considers the unique goals, challenges, and opportunities of each project. Defining the scope of the workshop, arranging logistics, and conducting thorough research beforehand are all critical components of a successful workshop.

Further Reading

If you want to dive deeper into the topic of facilitation and workshop moderation, here are some reading recommendations:

The Workshop Book: How to Design and Lead Successful Workshops by Pamela Hamilton

This book is a comprehensive guide to designing and leading effective workshops that can help teams to generate ideas, solve problems, and develop strategies.

Facilitating with Ease! Core Skills for Facilitators, Team Leaders and Members, Managers, Consultants, and Trainers by Ingrid Bens

This book provides a practical guide to the essential skills of facilitation, including managing group dynamics, facilitating consensus, and handling difficult situations.

Sprint: How to Solve Big Problems and Test New Ideas in Just Five Days by Jake Knapp, John Zeratsky, and Braden Kowitz

This book provides a practical guide to the five-day sprint process, which is a time-boxed, structured method for solving big problems and testing new ideas.

Business Model Generation: A Handbook for Visionaries, Game Changers, and Challengers by Alexander Osterwalder and Yves Pigneur

This book introduces the Business Model Canvas, a visual tool for designing, analyzing, and iterating on business models.

Value Proposition Design: How to Create Products and Services Customers Want by Alexander Osterwalder, Yves Pigneur, Gregory Bernarda, and Alan Smith

This book provides a practical guide to designing compelling value propositions that meet the needs of target customers.

The End of the Beginning: Wrapping Up Your Remote Collaboration Journey

Well done! You've completed 101 Remote Collaboration Hacks and have learned some valuable strategies for working with remote teams. We hope you've found the tips and tricks helpful and have already put them into practice.

But don't stop there! Keep learning, keep experimenting, and keep exploring. The world of remote collaboration is constantly evolving, and there are always new tools and techniques to discover.

To stay up to date with the latest trends in remote collaboration, head to innovation-hackers.de/links. There you'll find a wealth of resources and additional tools to help you collaborate more effectively with your remote teams. You can also contact us if you have any questions or feedback - we'd love to hear from you!

As a final call-to-action, we encourage you to continue putting what you've learned into practice. Remember, remote collaboration is not just about getting the work done, it's about building relationships, having fun, and supporting each other along the way.

Thank you for reading 101 Remote Collaboration Hacks. We hope you've enjoyed the journey and that the book has helped you become a better remote collaborator. Now go forth and collaborate like a boss!

Your Adam and Peter

Scan the QR code for an updated list of our favorite tools and links.

About the Authors

Together, Adam Egger and Peter Dern bring a wealth of experience and expertise to the table, making them well-suited to offer practical advice and insights on remote collaboration. They run a podcast together and have been writing newsletters about innovation, creativity, leadership, and decision-making.

Adam is an experienced expert in innovation strategy and organizational development with more than 20 years of experience in the IT industry. He has held various thought leadership positions at Software AG, where he has made significant contributions to the company's growth and success. Most recently he served as Global Head of Innovation Strategy and Organizational Development, where he has demonstrated an impressive ability to navigate complex challenges and drive meaningful change.

In addition to his professional achievements, Adam is also a passionate advocate for education. He dedicates his spare time to teaching communication, empathy, curiosity, and creativity to school kids. His commitment to education and community building has earned him widespread recognition and respect within the industry.

Peter is a highly experienced leader in the software industry, having held various leadership positions for over 20 years. His recent position was as Senior Vice President of Corporate Learning and People Development at Software AG, where he drove innovation, learning, and development. Prior to this, he managed customer-facing roles at SAP, overseeing education sales and delivery, and was responsible for complete education services delivery in Germany.

Peter is a highly motivated individual who believes in developing talent rather than just managing people. He is also a board member of the "European Association of Training Organizations" and frequently speaks at events and conferences on the topics of corporate learning and people development. His extensive background in leadership training, program development, and working with diverse teams makes him an excellent source of knowledge and practical advice on effective remote collaboration.

Adam and Peter have been conducting countless workshops and training sessions for employees, customers, and partners in the field of leadership and people management, innovation, user experience and customer centricity, in more than 70 countries worldwide over many years.

As the pandemic forced a shift to remote work, they swiftly adapted their training programs to offer their workshops and sessions fully virtual or in a hybrid setting. They developed new skills, which are shared in this book, enabling them to continue delivering high-quality training and support to individuals and organizations around the world.

What Adam Says About Peter

Peter is a perfect combination of knowledge and energy. You can talk to him about quantum physics or scream rock songs, and he will be equally enthusiastic. It is this blend of expertise and dynamism that makes him an exceptional trainer. I often wonder where he finds the energy to conduct multiple leadership training sessions every day - he is truly a rockstar!

For me he is the ultimate leadership guru. He has trained hundreds of executives worldwide, from board members to Level 1 managers, both in person and remotely. But that's not all - Peter's also a pitch and presentation training master. He's got experience in working with startups, including developing and implementing a startup program for his last company, Software AG.

I first met Peter around ten years ago during a storytelling training he ran. Even now, I remember his remarkable ability to simplify complex business concepts.

As the head of a learning and development department at a leading German IT company, Peter grants his employees the freedom and trust to thrive.

What Peter Says About Adam

Adam is the kind of guy who can take on any challenge and make it look like a piece of cake. He is a master at helping individuals and teams grow and innovate in the most effective and fun way possible. Seriously, have you ever seen someone address complex problems with such ease and creativity? It is utterly amazing.

In his free time, he teaches kids the skills they need to thrive in the future world - communication, empathy, curiosity, and creativity.

He is a minimalist living a good life, always focused on what truly matters. But that is not all - Adam is also a podcast junkie, always trying to learn something new. He is the epitome of curiosity, always looking for something new to explore. And when it comes to innovation, there is simply no one better. His methodology is super engaging, and he is always accessible, friendly, and empathetic with all cultures and personalities. He is an excellent coach and subject matter expert, with impeccable skills in understanding people and their body language.

But what really sets Adam apart is his ability to let others shine. He never puts himself before others and always encourages and inspires everyone around him to be their best selves. If you are ever in need of a growth mindset and transformational leader who can help you and your team perform and contribute at your highest level, look no further than Adam Egger. He is simply the best.

Acknowledgement

We would like to express our gratitude to the participants in our training sessions who have contributed significantly to the development of this book. It is through their engagement, enthusiasm, and valuable feedback that we have been able to refine our ideas and approach.

We have learned everything we know through and from them. Their willingness to share their experiences, insights, and learnings has been essential to shaping our thinking and ensuring that our content is relevant and impactful.

We would also like to thank our colleagues and mentors who have supported us throughout this journey. Your encouragement, guidance, and expertise have been invaluable.

We would also like to extend our sincere thanks to Bärbel, our editor, for her invaluable contribution in refining our ideas and ensuring that the book is readable and accessible.

Additionally, we would like to acknowledge the contributions of Rieke and Chris, two super creative young people who have helped us come up with many of the ideas in this book. Their fresh perspective and innovative thinking have been instrumental in shaping the book's content and style.

Finally, we extend our appreciation to our families and friends who were patient and understanding during the long weekend hours we spent working on this book. Your love and support have sustained us through the difficulties of the writing process.

Thank you all for being a part of this journey with us.

Quick Finder: All the Hacks

For your convenience we sorted all hacks into useful categories based on where and when to use each one.

Ideation, Creativity

#1: Have people note their ideas before collecting and processing them.
#25: Your mindset makes the difference: be positive, neutral, flexible, drive outcome, see the big picture and stay focused.
#38: Prioritize ideas using breakout groups.
#49: Use a virtual "parking lot" to capture ideas and questions that can be addressed later.
#64: Strictly separate divergent and convergent thinking.

Mindset

#2: Do not be the hero.
#12: Have a plan. But stay flexible.
#21: Your mindset makes the difference: be positive, neutral, flexible, drive outcome, see the big picture and stay focused.
#25: Your mindset makes the difference: be positive, neutral, flexible, drive outcome, see the big picture and stay focused.
#26: Stay positive, even if you have to fake it.
#101: Be authentic. Be you.

Breaking the ice, Connection

#3: Build connections before getting into content.
#18: Have the participants define who goes next in round robins like introductions.
#19: Create a safe space right from the start that everyone feels comfortable with.
#27: Break the ice for the introverts.
#39: Manage the energy flow.
#44: Use icebreakers. And use them often.
#69: Treat remote participants like VIPs in a talk show.
#72: Carefully plan warmup activities in hybrid settings to avoid the social cold start.
#99: Build connections that last.

Hacking the Tools

#4: Have a small but robust toolkit of exercises and techniques.

#9: Use your virtual background for content, not only for ambience.

#22: Use a timer in virtual environments to clearly indicate how much time is left during a break or an exercise.

#33: Get creative with camera perspectives and switch presenter modes frequently.

#45: Include a variety of interaction methods.

#46: Do not use PowerPoint.

#50: Use private communication channels to stay connected with co-facilitators and key stakeholders.

#52: Share virtual background images.

#54: Prefer easy-to-use tools and methods over sophisticated ones.

#74: Use paper and pencil in remote workshops.

#88: Check the technology.

#94: Clean up your desk, close unnecessary windows and turn off all notification pop-ups.

Your Desk

#61: Invest in a better microphone, camera, and lighting.

#62: Make sure you have a calm background.

Chat

#32: Use the chat as often as possible.

#40: Stay in the virtual workshop room after the session has ended.

#45: Include a variety of interaction methods.

#55: Harvest your valuable chat content.

#76: Use animated Gifs.

Whiteboards

#35: Keep the structure of your interim results on virtual whiteboards by copying the sticky notes instead of moving them around.

#56: Invest in creating impressive virtual whiteboards.

#60: Use warmup exercises to make participants familiar with your virtual whiteboard.

#70: Use virtual whiteboards also in hybrid sessions.

#80: Create your documentation while you do the workshop.

Music

#10: Play music.

#51: Use ambience music and sound carpets for silent work.

#66: Use sound effects.

Beginning

#5: No boring housekeeping rules at the beginning.

#8: Let everyone speak in the first minutes.

#13: If you run a session to solve problems, always start with "what's good", before you enter the problem space.

#18: Have the participants define who goes next in round robins like introductions.

#19: Create a safe space right from the start that everyone feels comfortable with.

#42: Start before you start. And start strong.

Breakouts

#6: Use breakout sessions in virtual workshops to increase the camera-on rate.

#14: Use breakout sessions in virtual workshops to raise the energy level.

#17: Five is the magic number for your virtual breakout sessions.

#38: Prioritize ideas using breakout groups.

#53: Give clear roles for breakout sessions.

#57: Provide perfectly precise and clear exercise descriptions for your breakout session.

#71: When using breakout rooms in hybrid settings, split up the locals into different rooms and mix them with the remote participants.

#78: Inform the participants before you close the breakout rooms.

#85: Give your teams enough time for their breakout sessions.

#87: Stay energized during breakout sessions with quick physical exercises.

#91: Do a quick check if all is fine after sending people to breakouts.

#93: Camera off when sneaking into a breakout room.

#98: Change the participants in subsequent Breakout Groups if you want to maximize creating new connections. And keep them the same if you need consistency and minimal distraction.

Preparation, Before

#7: Craft a compelling invitation.

#24: Never forget to check the logistics. In as much detail as possible.

#31: Use a co-facilitator.

#36: Prepare. Prepare. And then: prepare again.

#41: No assumptions!

#48: Invite your critics.

#58: Have a backup plan for technical issues.

#63: Augment the virtual reality to the desks of your participants.

#77: Meet your client in person. At least once.

#88: Check the technology.

#89: Do not rely on pre-reading for your workshops.

#96: Use a living script to keep control of the timing.

Breaks

#22: Use a timer in virtual environments to clearly indicate how much time is left during a break or an exercise.

#43: Plan enough (short) breaks.

#79: Have lunch together.

End

#23: Ensure everyone leaves the workshop feeling they accomplished something.

#40: Stay in the virtual workshop room after the session has ended.

#47: End on a high.

#86: Avoid tedious round robin debriefing sessions after breakout exercises.

#90: Skip the homework after a workshop or in between sessions.

#97: Ensure proper follow-up activities.

Communication

#7: Craft a compelling invitation.

#9: Use your virtual background for content, not only for ambience.

#11: Do not share the agenda with the time allotted for each section or part with the participants.

#15: Play YouTube videos during breaks.

#19: Create a safe space right from the start that everyone feels comfortable with.

#23: Ensure everyone leaves the workshop feeling they accomplished something.

#28: Use body language in virtual workshops to create specific moods.

#29: Demo your exercises, do not only explain them.

#37: Manage your stakeholders - continuously.

#50: Use private communication channels to stay connected with co-facilitators and key stakeholders.

#55: Harvest your valuable chat content.

#65: Don't share a link before you explain what will happen when people click on it.

#75: Be mindful about language barriers and use available tools and creative exercises formats to overcome this.

#81: Engage your audience by returning questions to them.

#83: Allow moments of silence.

#95: Look into the camera lens if you want to look into the eyes of your participants.

#100: Avoid lengthy feedback rounds at the end. And use one-sentence feedback in the chat and formal surveys for real insight.

Problems

#37: Manage your stakeholders - continuously.

#58: Have a backup plan for technical issues.

#59: Have a backup plan for unreliable participants.

#84: Observe your audience and watch out for the flickering effect.

Appearance

#28: Use body language in virtual workshops to create specific moods.

#30: Make sure you are dressed appropriately.

Agenda

#11: Do not share the agenda with the time allotted for each section or part with the participants.

#16: Separate between problem definition and solution finding. Problems first, solutions second.

Videos

#15: Play YouTube videos during breaks.

#73: Show your clients what they will get using video demos.

Structure

#16: Separate between problem definition and solution finding. Problems first, solutions second.

#20: Spend a lot more time discussing the problem than the solution.

Hybrid

#67: Avoid hybrid events.

#68: Never run hybrid sessions alone. Use a co-facilitator to manage the onsite team.

#70: Use virtual whiteboards also in hybrid sessions.

#71: When using breakout rooms in hybrid settings, split up the locals into different rooms and mix them with the remote participants.

#72: Carefully plan warmup activities in hybrid settings to avoid the social cold start.

Presentation

#9: Use your virtual background for content, not only for ambience.

#82: Do not use static content.

#92: Limit your teaching slots to the unavoidable minimum.

Index

Impressum

Title: 101 Remote Collaboration Hacks

Authors:
Adam Egger
Herta Mansbacher Str.171
64289 Darmstadt

Dr. Peter Dern
An der Brennerei 15
69231 Rauenberg

Publisher:	Self-Published via KDP
ISBN:	979-8391328544
Cover design:	Olayemi Bolaji
Editor:	Bärbel Strothmann-Schmitt
Graphics:	Franzi Manko – linkedin.com/in/franzi-manko

For more information about this book, please visit
www.innovation-hackers.de/links
For questions or inquiries about bulk purchases, please contact the authors at info@innovation-hackers.de.

Disclaimer: The information provided in this book is for educational and entertainment purposes only. The authors do not warrant or represent that the information in this book is accurate, complete, or suitable for any purpose. The authors shall not be liable for any damages or injuries arising from the use of this book.